MODERN WORLD LEADERS

Angela Merkel

MODERN WORLD LEADERS

Michelle Bachelet
Tony Blair
George W. Bush
Hugo Chávez
Jacques Chirac
Hu Jintao
Hamid Karzai
Ali Khamenei
Thabo Mbeki
Angela Merkel
Hosni Mubarak
Pervez Musharraf
Pope Benedict XVI
Pope John Paul II
Vladimir Putin
The Saudi Royal Family
Ariel Sharon
Viktor Yushchenko

MODERN WORLD LEADERS

Angela Merkel

Clifford W. Mills

CHELSEA HOUSE
PUBLISHERS
An imprint of Infobase Publishing

Angela Merkel

Chelsea House
An imprint of Infobase Publishing
132 West 31st Street
New York, NY 10001

Library of Congress Cataloging-in-Publication Data

Mills, Cliff, 1947-
  Angela Merkel / Clifford W. Mills.
     p. cm. — (Modern world leaders)
  Includes bibliographical references and index.
  ISBN-13: 978-0-7910-9496-9 (hardcover)
  ISBN-10: 0-7910-9496-0 (hardcover)
  1. Merkel, Angela, 1954—Juvenile literature. 2. Heads of state—Germany—Biography—
Juvenile literature. 3. Germany—Politics and government—1990- I. Title. II. Series.
  DD290.33.M47M55 2007
  943.088'3092—dc22
  [B]   2007000967

Chelsea House books are available at special discounts when purchased in bulk quantities
for businesses, associations, institutions, or sales promotions. Please call our Special Sales
Department in New York at (212) 967-8800 or (800) 322-8755.

You can find Chelsea House on the World Wide Web at http://www.chelseahouse.com

Text design by Erik Lindstrom
Cover design by Takeshi Takahashi

Printed in the United States of America

Bang EJB 10 9 8 7 6 5 4 3 2 1

This book is printed on acid-free paper.

All links and Web addresses were checked and verified to be correct at the time
of publication. Because of the dynamic nature of the Web, some addresses and links
may have changed since publication and may no longer be valid.

TABLE OF CONTENTS

Arthur M. Schlesinger, Jr.

On Leadership

Leadership, it may be said, is really what makes the world go round. Love no doubt smoothes the passage; but love is a private transaction between consenting adults. Leadership is a public transaction with history. The idea of leadership affirms the capacity of individuals to move, inspire, and mobilize masses of people so that they act together in pursuit of an end. Sometimes leadership serves good purposes, sometimes bad; but whether the end is benign or evil, great leaders are those men and women who leave their personal stamp on history.

Now, the very concept of leadership implies the proposition that individuals can make a difference. This proposition has never been universally accepted. From classical times to the present day, eminent thinkers have regarded individuals as no more than the agents and pawns of larger forces, whether the gods and goddesses of the ancient world or, in the modern era, race, class, nation, the dialectic, the will of the people, the spirit of the times, history itself. Against such forces, the individual dwindles into insignificance.

So contends the thesis of historical determinism. Tolstoy's great novel *War and Peace* offers a famous statement of the case. Why, Tolstoy asked, did millions of men in the Napoleonic Wars, denying their human feelings and their common sense, move back and forth across Europe slaughtering their fellows? "The war," Tolstoy answered, "was bound to happen simply because it was bound to happen." All prior history determined it. As for leaders, they, Tolstoy said, "are but the labels that serve to give a name to an end and, like labels, they have the least possible connection with the event." The greater the leader, "the more conspicuous the inevitability and the predestination of every act he commits." The leader, said Tolstoy, is "the slave of history."

Determinism takes many forms. Marxism is the determinism of class. Nazism the determinism of race. But the idea of men and women as the slaves of history runs athwart the deepest human instincts. Rigid determinism abolishes the idea of human freedom—the assumption of free choice that underlies every move we make, every word we speak, every thought we think. It abolishes the idea of human responsibility, since it is manifestly unfair to reward or punish people for actions that are by definition beyond their control. No one can live consistently by any deterministic creed. The Marxist states prove this themselves by their extreme susceptibility to the cult of leadership.

More than that, history refutes the idea that individuals make no difference. In December 1931, a British politician crossing Fifth Avenue in New York City between 76th and 77th streets around 10:30 P.M. looked in the wrong direction and was knocked down by an automobile—a moment, he later recalled, of a man aghast, a world aglare: "I do not understand why I was not broken like an eggshell or squashed like a gooseberry." Fourteen months later an American politician, sitting in an open car in Miami, Florida, was fired on by an assassin; the man beside him was hit. Those who believe that individuals make no difference to history might well ponder whether the next two decades would have been the same had Mario Constasino's car killed Winston Churchill in 1931 and Giuseppe Zangara's bullet killed Franklin Roosevelt in 1933. Suppose, in addition, that Lenin had died of typhus in Siberia in 1895 and that Hitler had been killed on the western front in 1916. What would the twentieth century have looked like now?

For better or for worse, individuals do make a difference. "The notion that a people can run itself and its affairs anonymously," wrote the philosopher William James, "is now well known to be the silliest of absurdities. Mankind does nothing save through initiatives on the part of inventors, great or small, and imitation by the rest of us—these are the sole factors in human progress. Individuals of genius show the way, and set the patterns, which common people then adopt and follow."

Leadership, James suggests, means leadership in thought as well as in action. In the long run, leaders in thought may well make the greater difference to the world. "The ideas of economists and political philosophers, both when they are right and when they are wrong," wrote John Maynard Keynes, "are more powerful than is commonly understood. Indeed the world is ruled by little else. Practical men, who believe themselves to be quite exempt from any intellectual influences, are usually the slaves of some defunct economist. . . . The power of vested interests is vastly exaggerated compared with the gradual encroachment of ideas."

But, as Woodrow Wilson once said, "Those only are leaders of men, in the general eye, who lead in action. . . . It is at their hands that new thought gets its translation into the crude language of deeds." Leaders in thought often invent in solitude and obscurity, leaving to later generations the tasks of imitation. Leaders in action—the leaders portrayed in this series—have to be effective in their own time.

And they cannot be effective by themselves. They must act in response to the rhythms of their age. Their genius must be adapted, in a phrase from William James, "to the receptivities of the moment." Leaders are useless without followers. "There goes the mob," said the French politician, hearing a clamor in the streets. "I am their leader. I must follow them." Great leaders turn the inchoate emotions of the mob to purposes of their own. They seize on the opportunities of their time, the hopes, fears, frustrations, crises, potentialities. They succeed when events have prepared the way for them, when the community is awaiting to be aroused, when they can provide the clarifying and organizing ideas. Leadership completes the circuit between the individual and the mass and thereby alters history.

It may alter history for better or for worse. Leaders have been responsible for the most extravagant follies and most monstrous crimes that have beset suffering humanity. They have also been vital in such gains as humanity has made in individual freedom, religious and racial tolerance, social justice, and respect for human rights.

There is no sure way to tell in advance who is going to lead for good and who for evil. But a glance at the gallery of men and women in MODERN WORLD LEADERS suggests some useful tests.

One test is this: Do leaders lead by force or by persuasion? By command or by consent? Through most of history leadership was exercised by the divine right of authority. The duty of followers was to defer and to obey. "Theirs not to reason why/Theirs but to do and die." On occasion, as with the so-called enlightened despots of the eighteenth century in Europe, absolutist leadership was animated by humane purposes. More often, absolutism nourished the passion for domination, land, gold, and conquest and resulted in tyranny.

The great revolution of modern times has been the revolution of equality. "Perhaps no form of government," wrote the British historian James Bryce in his study of the United States, *The American Commonwealth*, "needs great leaders so much as democracy." The idea that all people should be equal in their legal condition has undermined the old structure of authority, hierarchy, and deference. The revolution of equality has had two contrary effects on the nature of leadership. For equality, as Alexis de Tocqueville pointed out in his great study *Democracy in America*, might mean equality in servitude as well as equality in freedom.

"I know of only two methods of establishing equality in the political world," Tocqueville wrote. "Rights must be given to every citizen, or none at all to anyone . . . save one, who is the master of all." There was no middle ground "between the sovereignty of all and the absolute power of one man." In his astonishing prediction of twentieth-century totalitarian dictatorship, Tocqueville explained how the revolution of equality could lead to the *Führerprinzip* and more terrible absolutism than the world had ever known.

But when rights are given to every citizen and the sovereignty of all is established, the problem of leadership takes a new form, becomes more exacting than ever before. It is easy to issue commands and enforce them by the rope and the stake, the concentration camp and the *gulag*. It is much harder to use argument and achievement to overcome opposition and win consent. The Founding Fathers of the United States understood the difficulty. They believed that history had given them the opportunity to decide, as Alexander Hamilton wrote in the first Federalist Paper, whether men are indeed capable of basing government on "reflection and choice, or whether they are forever destined to depend . . . on accident and force."

Government by reflection and choice called for a new style of leadership and a new quality of followership. It required leaders to be responsive to popular concerns, and it required followers to be active and informed participants in the process. Democracy does not eliminate emotion from politics; sometimes it fosters demagoguery; but it is confident that, as the greatest of democratic leaders put it, you cannot fool all of the people all of the time. It measures leadership by results and retires those who overreach or falter or fail.

It is true that in the long run despots are measured by results too. But they can postpone the day of judgment, sometimes indefinitely, and in the meantime they can do infinite harm. It is also true that democracy is no guarantee of virtue and intelligence in government, for the voice of the people is not necessarily the voice of God. But democracy, by assuring the right of opposition, offers built-in resistance to the evils inherent in absolutism. As the theologian Reinhold Niebuhr summed it up, "Man's capacity for justice makes democracy possible, but man's inclination to justice makes democracy necessary."

A second test for leadership is the end for which power is sought. When leaders have as their goal the supremacy of a master race or the promotion of totalitarian revolution or the acquisition and exploitation of colonies or the protection of greed and privilege or the preservation of personal power, it is likely that their leadership will do little to advance the cause of humanity. When their goal is the abolition of slavery, the liberation of women, the enlargement of opportunity for the poor and powerless, the extension of equal rights to racial minorities, the defense of the freedoms of expression and opposition, it is likely that their leadership will increase the sum of human liberty and welfare.

Leaders have done great harm to the world. They have also conferred great benefits. You will find both sorts in this series. Even "good" leaders must be regarded with a certain wariness. Leaders are not demigods; they put on their trousers one leg after another just like ordinary mortals. No leader is infallible, and every leader needs to be reminded of this at regular intervals. Irreverence irritates leaders but is their salvation. Unquestioning submission corrupts leaders and demeans followers. Making a cult of a leader is always a mistake. Fortunately hero worship generates its own antidote. "Every hero," said Emerson, "becomes a bore at last."

The single benefit the great leaders confer is to embolden the rest of us to live according to our own best selves, to be active, insistent, and resolute in affirming our own sense of things. For great leaders attest to the reality of human freedom against the supposed inevitabilities of history. And they attest to the wisdom and power that may lie within the most unlikely of us, which is why Abraham Lincoln remains the supreme example of great leadership. A great leader, said Emerson, exhibits new possibilities to all humanity. "We feed on genius. . . . Great men exist that there may be greater men."

Great leaders, in short, justify themselves by emancipating and empowering their followers. So humanity struggles to master its destiny, remembering with Alexis de Tocqueville: "It is true that around every man a fatal circle is traced beyond which he cannot pass; but within the wide verge of that circle he is powerful and free; as it is with man, so with communities." ●

1

Finding Freedom

TURNING POINTS IN MODERN HISTORY CAN BE CATASTROPHIC EVENTS, SUCH as 9/11, or joyous events, such as 11/9. Much of the world is familiar with the date 9/11. Many do not know or remember what happened on 11/9.

On a cold November evening in 1989, an East German official in Berlin named Günter Schabowski called a televised news conference. For almost an hour he read a long statement that meant very little to the few journalists listening. Some of the journalists tuned out. Others were tired of endless bureaucratic pronouncements from the East German talking heads, but kept listening out of duty and habit. Near the end of the prepared statement, Schabowski read a small note that said that travel from East Berlin to West Berlin was now allowed. Everyone thought they had misheard what he said. The journalists looked at each other in confusion. No questions

In this August 13, 1961, photo, East German soldiers construct barbed wire barricades to restrict travel between East Berlin and West Berlin. West Berlin townspeople observe the process. Eventually, this barricade became a 12-foot-high wall of concrete and steel, and prevented passage between the two areas for nearly 30 years.

were allowed. That simple statement, however, set off a tidal wave of world events that is still being felt today.

THE BERLIN WALL

Since the end of World War II, Germany had been divided into two countries: East Germany and West Germany. Its capital,

The Wall grew like a monster as layers and layers of brick were added over time, along with more barbed wire.

Berlin, had also been divided into East and West. The two superpowers responsible for the division, the United States (and its allies) and the Soviet Union, wrestled for power over the country and the world. The United States and its allies helped rebuild West Germany and West Berlin, and the Soviet Union controlled East Germany and East Berlin.

Berlin was a problem for both sides. The capital city was located almost 100 miles inside the German Democratic Republic (GDR), as East Germany was officially known. The two worldviews clashed most directly in the city due to different economies. It was soon clear that more jobs were being created in West Berlin, since businesses had more freedom to start up and grow. Many East Berliners began to move to West Berlin for its greater freedom and better jobs, and the flow of emigrants became an embarrassment for the Soviet Union and East Germany. The leaders felt they had to do something to save face. They were in a struggle for hearts and minds, and they were losing.

In a brutally efficient 24-hour operation that began on the night of August 12, 1961, Soviet soldiers sealed off East Berlin subways and train stations, tore up the streets, and began to build a 12-foot high wall of concrete and steel, which was topped with barbed wire and machine guns. The wall divided the city of Berlin, and no travel was allowed between East and West any longer. The Soviet Union and East Germany had solved the emigration problem in Berlin the only way they knew how.

Suddenly, 60,000 workers could no longer get to their jobs. The wall divided families. Lifelong friends were destined not to see each other again for the next 28 years. The Berlin wall became a symbol of tyranny and oppression. The planned economies and rigidly structured lives of those living under Communist rule in East Germany and in the Soviet Union seemed to be summed up in that one physical barrier. Over 250 people lost their lives trying desperately to climb it and reach the freedom that was only yards away. People on the western side could hear gunshots and cries from the eastern side.

The wall eventually extended for 97 miles around Berlin and its surroundings. Some sections of it were later fitted with state-of-the-art automatic weapons run by motion detectors that shot at anything that moved. The wall grew like a monster as layers and layers of brick were added over time, along with more barbed wire. The ground around it became a dead zone, a death stripe. When U.S. president Ronald Reagan famously urged the Soviet leader Mikhail Gorbachev in 1987 to tear down the wall, few expected that it would happen.

A YOUNG WOMAN CHANGED FOREVER

The Schabowski news conference was televised in West Berlin only, but many people in East Berlin had televisions that could pick up signals intended only for the West. A young woman in East Berlin named Angela Merkel had been watching, but she was relaxing after her weekly session at her favorite sauna and was not really paying attention. She wondered if she had heard correctly that travel was now permitted. Surely such a world-shaking announcement would not come in a comment after an hour of talking. Merkel called her mother and blurted out, "If the wall ever falls down, we will go to the Kempinski and eat lobsters!" (Since the Kempinski was West Berlin's fanciest hotel, they had long dreamed of how wonderful a night there would be.)

One of Merkel's first memories was of her mother crying in church as the wall was being built. Her mother had known what hardship was to follow. Their lives in East Germany had been harsh and without luxuries. The family had at one time milked goats and cooked soup from stinging nettles to survive. Dinner at the Kempinski (only a few blocks away) seemed an impossible dream.

Merkel then did what many East Berliners did. She went outside and walked quickly to the nearest wall checkpoint to test the guards, to see if what she thought she heard was true. She must have expected to see tanks and the dreaded guards with their cold eyes and hard boots, as always. She approached the checkpoint tentatively with a few other people, and they were shocked when, instead of shooting, the guards allowed them all to walk right into the western sector. The East Germans entered a whole new world, a world with more color and life. Some would later say the first thing they saw was all the graffiti and art on the western side of the wall. Their side had nothing but warnings and faded bloodstains.

As the news spread, a small stream of people became a deliriously joyful rushing torrent. West Berliners flocked to each checkpoint to meet brothers and sisters, fathers and mothers. East Berliners pushed through the checkpoints, rushing into spontaneous reunions. Families clutched each other for the first time in a lifetime. Then, some younger East Germans started climbing onto the wall and tearing at it. First they used their bare hands and then they found hammers to batter away at the long-standing symbol of tyranny. West Berliners joined them in cutting down the barbed wire and hacking away at the concrete with sledge hammers and iron bars. These were the first acts of a joyful unification.

Today, only a few sections of the wall still stand. The most visible evidence of its existence is a red line or a double row of cobblestones where it once stood, winding through dozens of Berlin's streets. Tourists too young to have seen the wall often have a hard time imagining its soul-deadening powers. Souvenir fragments of the wall are found all over the

After German officials raised the ban on travel between East Berlin and West Berlin, images of German citizens climbing the wall—and eventually destroying it—flooded newspapers, magazines, and TV news and captivated people around the world. Many Germans had never been to the other side of the city, and others were able to reunite with family and friends they hadn't seen in 30 years.

world, including in museums and U.S. government buildings. They are reminders of 11/9.

With the tearing down of the wall, much of the Communist world also began to crumble. The decades-long struggle between individual liberty and collective repression known as the Cold War was coming to an end. There were no fireworks or parades in East Berlin on that night of November 9, 1989, but for every 11/9 afterward in Germany there would be celebrations of what has been called the happiest day in German history. A tidal wave of freedom and joy had broken over the wall and rushed throughout the countryside.

NOVEMBER 22, 2005: THE NEW CHANCELLOR

Angela Merkel and her mother have still not been to the Kempinski for lobsters. Merkel has been too busy. Her life changed the instant she walked through the wall. She has since told reporters that "the biggest surprise of my life was freedom. I expected the wall. I did not expect freedom. . . . Once you've had such a wonderful surprise in your life, then you think anything is possible." Suddenly, Angela Merkel's life was filled with possibilities.

One of the remotest possibilities must have been that the shy and scholarly physicist with little interest in politics would rise to hold the highest office in Germany—chancellor. German politics had been ruled by men from West Germany for as long as anyone could remember. A woman from East Germany was doubly different from what people were used to in government. Wealthy men who had interests in law and power rose to the top, not poor women with interests in science and foreign languages. Merkel had wanted to become a teacher of either science or language, but was forbidden by the East German system because her father was a Lutheran pastor. Children of religious parents were not allowed to take on certain professions in atheistic East Germany.

A memorial strip now marks the site where the Berlin wall once stood. Three sections of the wall are still standing and serve as memorials. Today, pieces of the wall are sold as souvenirs.

Until the night of 11/9, Merkel seemed to have very little interest in political life, but she soon developed a very intense one. In a few short years, she would be placing memorial wreaths at the foot of the existing remnants of the Berlin wall, and giving speeches about freedom and opportunity.

Angela Merkel rose to the top of a male-oriented, conservative, and traditional political party called the Christian Democratic Union (CDU). She was smarter and worked harder than almost everyone in the party. She said what she did and did what she said. She was a rarity in politics. She didn't tell people what they wanted to hear; she told them what she thought she could do to solve political problems. She listened, and she tried to get people to finds areas of agreement and work from there. Her years in East Germany taught her how powerful government could be, and she was determined to use that power to serve others and not control them.

She heard stinging criticism about her looks, her hair, her speaking voice, her clothes, and her divorce and remarriage. She heard critics tell her she should be at home having babies and taking care of her house. Women from her own hometown of Templin said they would never vote for her because her priorities were not theirs. Her second husband wants no part of her career, refusing to become the smiling spouse looking up adoringly during speeches given for the hundredth time.

Despite all the forces working against her, Angela Merkel was elected by the German parliament to become chancellor on November 22, 2005. Of the 614 Parliament members, 397 voted for her, and she was sworn in as the eighth chancellor since the end of World War II. She is the first woman ever to lead Germany. She has traveled to Washington, D.C., Moscow, London, Paris, Beijing, and many other places to work for Germany, the European Union countries, and the world. She has become a voice of reason and intelligence not seen enough today in world politics. Hers is one of the most remarkable stories among world leaders, and it begins with her parents in the city of Hamburg.

2

Growing Up in a World Divided

HORST KASNER IS A POWERFUL AND DYNAMIC MAN. HE WAS BORN IN Berlin, Germany, on August 6, 1926, and grew up watching the horrors of World War II. No German escaped the ravages of the war. Kasner became convinced that a career as a Protestant minister would help bring peace back to his life, and perhaps he could even help bring some healing to a torn-up country. He was idealistic and young. His religious studies eventually took him to the international city of Hamburg, Germany, on the Elbe River and near the North Sea. Hundreds of years ago, Hamburg had been one of the first European cities to embrace the reforms of Martin Luther, the founder of Protestantism. Because of that, the city had several universities as well as several schools of theology. Young Kasner attended one of them, and was an intense and thorough student, drawn to the evangelical side of the Protestant church.

Unlike Catholic priests, Protestant ministers were allowed to marry, and Kasner had wed a young woman named Herlind Jentzsch. She had grown up in Danzig, Germany, and had always wanted to be a teacher. Herlind was two years younger than Kasner, and she too was intelligent and intense. In Hamburg, she taught Latin and English to many levels of students. Languages had always interested her, and living in Hamburg—where many cultures come together—provided her with plenty of students to teach and learn from. Herlind knew that the city had a rich history from its position at the intersection of several trade routes. It had been destroyed first by Vikings and then by fires and finally by the bombs of World War II. It was rebuilt each time as a bigger and more vibrant place with more people speaking more languages.

The Kasners knew they wanted to start a family and soon did so. Their first child was born in the middle of the hot summer of 1954, on July 17. They decided to name her Angela Dorothea. As a new father, Kasner started looking for work as a pastor in the Lutheran Church. A position was offered, but not in West Germany. Angela Dorothea Kasner was only six weeks old when her family's life changed suddenly and completely.

BECOMING EAST GERMANS

Germany had been divided into East and West for a few years, but the flow of East Germans to West Germany was steadily increasing. Mr. Kasner decided that he wanted and needed to take a ministry near his home city of Berlin, in East Germany, despite the fact that so many Germans were moving west to escape Communist rule. He may have felt he was more needed under the East German regime. Socialist and Communist countries have been notoriously hostile to religion. The state, not religion, is the highest authority under Communist rule, and few challenges to state authority were ever made by anyone, even the church.

Four-year-old Angela Kasner poses for a photograph in a German forest in 1958. When she was just a young girl, Angela was taken out of West Germany by her parents to live in Communist East Germany. It was a move that would change her life, and would give her a unique perspective when leading the country.

Mr. Kasner contacted a moving company to take the family from Hamburg to a small village named Quitzow, about 50 miles north of Berlin. He had been assigned a parish there, and needed to begin work soon. The mover was astonished; he said there were two kinds of people who went to East Germany from the West: Communists and idiots. Mr. Kasner asked which category the man felt the Kasners fell into. The mover replied he would form a third category. He didn't say what he would call that group. So, Angela became one of the few people who could say she was born in West Germany and grew up in East Germany. She was already different from most others.

The family soon moved out of the parsonage house at the church to live in the nearby town of Templin. This small city of more than 17,000 people is in the German federal state of Brandenburg. Germany has 16 federal states in all. Brandenburg was considered to be at the very heart of East Germany. It was like most German towns, a very ordered and regulated place. Templin is now a spa and resort town, an escape for Berliners. Its glacial lakes and green forests surround a very old town center with intact walls from its days as a medieval village. It was a scenic and safe place to grow up, at least to the eyes of a child.

THE EARLY CDU

When Angela's brother Marcus was born on July 7, 1957, she was old enough to know that she was suddenly no longer the only child. She seemed, however, to have welcomed her new baby brother. Soon, she would get to order her brother around. She must have had some mixed feelings about being replaced as the center of attention. Though she has not publicly discussed her childhood very much, her German biographer, Gerd Langguth, has interviewed a number of her schoolmates. All report that she had a normal and happy early childhood. She spoke her first words at an early age, but did not walk until much later. She confessed to another biographer, Patricia Lessnerkraus:

I was a sheer idiot when it came to moving. My parents had to explain how to walk downhill, from a purely technical point of view. Something that a normal person can do automatically I had to think about in my mind and practice.

So, she was awkward and unathletic at a young age. She didn't seem to like being the center of attention. She was shy, and found reading a good way to escape.

By all accounts, her father was very strict with his children, and Angela must have felt an extra pressure to behave well and later perform well in school because her father was a minister. Her father and her mother demanded much of her, and it seems she demanded a lot from herself. Angela wanted to be more than competent in anything she did. She wanted to be the best.

Church attendance was not banned in East Germany, but children of clergy were discriminated against in many ways. Many people seemed to wait for them to fail in anything they did. So, as soon as she entered school, Angela worked hard at her studies and behaved cautiously. She also had a remarkable memory. At a very early age, she could instantly recall all the names of people in East and West German government positions. She may not have had much of an interest in politics, but she seems to have paid at least some attention at an early age to those in power.

She was drawn to languages, science, and mathematics. Former classmates describe her with her nose in a book, studying even while waiting for the school bus. She did not seem very interested in boys, unlike some of her classmates in the early grades. For years, she was a member of the CDU—the Club der Ungeküssten, or "Club of the Unkissed." Her former math teacher Hans Ulrich Beestow says she tried not to be a nerd, however. She was so good in school that other students often tried to copy her homework and she often let them. No one knows if she was the kind of student who made sure the

"THIS WISH TO BE BETTER THAN OTHERS WAS OBVIOUSLY AT WORK IN ANGELA MERKEL VERY EARLY . . ."

—Gerd Langguth

class got homework every night, but she was usually at the top of her class.

German schools at the time tended to encourage competition between students, rather than cooperation. The best and the brightest would go to university later, a position reserved for only a few. Angela competed in math and science meets as she got older, and proved herself a very high-achieving and high-powered student. Biographer Gerd Langguth comments on this phase of her life:

> This wish to be better than others was obviously at work in Angela Merkel very early—and at school she was, as a former teacher says, an "exception," an "ideal pupil." In all her subjects (except sport) she achieved extremely good grades, yet at the same time was not looked upon as a "grind." . . . She was rather inconspicuous, which was connected to another elementary rule which she was taught by her parents: Never draw attention to yourself.

She did not spend all of her time studying, however. Family photos show her cooking after a sailing trip when she was young, and playing compulsory volleyball as well. Templin provided many places for nature walks and bicycle rides. Angela loved riding her bike, although she tells of having three of them stolen. Somehow, her parents managed to replace them. She also was bitten by a dog when she was young, causing a lifelong dislike of them. So, like most, her childhood had its share of small misfortunes.

East Germans were required to have daily physical exercise in school, and those showing real athletic promise were often sent to special training facilities. Angela was not one of the special athletes, but she later showed the world how interested she was in soccer. She also later pursued hiking and jogging as a way to get away from all her concerns, and her love of walking started early.

When her sister Irene was born on August 19, 1964, Angela had just turned 10 years old and could help raise her baby sister. Mrs. Kasner had been unable to get a job teaching, since spouses of clergy were also discriminated against in East Germany. The family of five was able to survive without many luxuries. Soup was often a main course. An East German pastor was poorly paid, making less than most factory workers. The family eventually had two cars, however, which was unusual for a minister's family in a small town. Families usually had to wait many years for a basic car, called a Trabant. The family also had a well-stocked library, with many books from relatives in West Germany. This was also unusual for an East German family. The Kasners were poor in some ways, and rich in others.

THE CHURCH IN SOCIALISM

Mr. Kasner's duties as minister gradually changed. He became the head of the *Pastoralkolleg* ("Pastoral College") in Templin, a training center for Protestant ministers. The center also included a building where children with special needs were cared for and educated. He had a demanding and difficult job. He was also becoming a force in a movement known eventually as "the church in socialism." Some East German ministers and priests were trying to work with the government to allow for more acceptance of church values and church attendance. Kasner remained a believer in the socialist and Marxist idea that wealth needed to be distributed among people more evenly than capitalism would allow. But he also believed that the church could play a role in socialism, preaching acceptance of and faith in God as part of being a good socialist citizen. He taught that the two belief systems, socialism and religious faith, could co-exist. People could be loyal to both at the same time.

The East German leaders, headed at the time by Deputy Premier Walter Ulbricht, began to tolerate the church more and not try to ban it. In the early 1950s, the Socialist Unity Party (in German, the SED, an abbreviation for "Sozialistische Einheitspartei Deutschlands") had fought against the influence of the church, but many people had resisted giving up their faith. So the East German leaders stopped aggressively fighting religion about the time Kasner took over his ministry. They felt that religion would probably disappear once the East German society became more mature. Only the older citizens would cling to their belief in God, the leaders must have thought. They would allow certain churches to exist, as long as they did not preach any sort of rebellion against the state.

Communism and socialism would later be seen by many as blind to the real needs of human nature. Some would comment years later that communism was the organized prevention of whatever came naturally. Others argued that a good idea—the redistribution of wealth so all could have a good life—was at war with another even better idea—human freedom. Sometimes in world history tragedy comes from good ideas warring with other good ideas, not good warring with evil. Unfortunately, socialism and communism in practice tended to equalize scarcity and suffering, not wealth and happiness. But, in the 1950s in East Germany, social order and security were all that seemed important to its leaders. They believed in a system that would lose in a struggle with democracy, but no one knew that then.

Kasner was a member of a loose organization called the Weissenseer Circle. This group of intellectuals discussed many of the issues related to religious freedom and governmental control of religion. The group had some support in the East German government. They also, however, had

Angela Kasner lived in this house in the East German town of Templin from 1957 to 1973. Angela's father headed up the training center for protestant ministers.

people who would come close to criticizing the East German regime for being too repressive. Many historians point out that with Kasner's help, the Evangelical Church became more tolerated by the East German government. Several church leaders were granted acceptance of public services of worship, permits to build new churches, and given some favors. Some pastors in the Weissenseer Working Group (as it was also called) were more likely to have cars, a rarity in a socialist state for church leaders at the time. They were also allowed to travel under special circumstances, and some became important in organizing prisoner exchanges with West Germany. A small but important line of communication between East and West Germany remained open through these particular church leaders.

The Kasners met many people who came through Templin as part of the training center and the Weissenseer Circle. These were smart and educated people, some of whom would later become leaders in the East and West Germany unification process. Some of them, however, were spies. Like most East German citizens, the Kasner family was being watched.

THE STASI IS WATCHING

The German Democratic Republic (East Germany) wanted control over its citizens. It knew the best way to control people was to have information about them and use that information to force them to be loyal and patriotic. East Germany set up one of the world's most complete and effective spying operations over its own citizens. The Stasi (from *Staatssicherheit*) was a security and intelligence network based in East Berlin. It had nearly 100,000 full-time employees, and used about 300,000 informants. The informants were ordinary people recruited to spy on their fellow citizens, reporting anything that might be interpreted as anti–East German thought or behavior. The Stasi kept some 6 million files. Since East Germany had a population of roughly 16 million, that meant that more than one-third of the population was under suspicion.

The Stasi kept a close eye on anyone whom they thought might be subversive. All phone calls to West Germany were monitored, as was all mail. Most factories and companies had people spying on their fellow workers. Family members were sometimes asked to spy on other family members, and, if they refused, they were punished in a variety of ways, including imprisonment.

The Kasners were watched by the Stasi because they were part of the church. Captured Stasi files after the fall of

the Berlin wall show that Mr. Kasner was approached by the
Stasi to become a spy after he taught students about Andrei
Sakharov. Sakharov was a Russian scientist who helped develop
the Russian hydrogen bomb, but then became an activist for
peace. He wanted a ban on nuclear weapons and more freedom
in the Communist Soviet Union. Kasner crossed a forbidden
line when he introduced students to Sakharov's letters. The
Stasi called Kasner in to an office in Berlin and told him it was
forbidden to discuss such things. They said that if he worked
for the Stasi, he would not be punished. Kasner refused to
cooperate. He told them people could hear Sakharov's views on
the radio.

Angela was asked soon after to become part of the Stasi.
Perhaps frustrated that they had not been able to recruit her
father, they now concentrated on his oldest child. Angela's file
shows she told the Stasi she was "a chatterbox" and could not
keep secrets. She said she would make a poor spy. She didn't
seem to be punished for her noncooperation, but knowing the
Stasi was always nearby had to make a profound impression
on a young person. Big Brother was watching. She would now
and later learn to keep her real thoughts to herself, to create a
private world that was separate from a public and political one.
Her parents had taught her this as well, but dealing with the
Stasi probably reinforced this teaching. Later, reporters would
note that she could talk a good deal about herself but never
reveal anything. She was a politician in the making.

THE STASI IN HISTORY

The secret police of the GDR had a motto, "Shield and Sword of
the Party." As a shield, it protected the party from criticism. As a
sword, it punished people the party did not like or agree with.

The Stasi was founded on February 8, 1950, and was mod-
eled on the Soviet Union's KGB. Its methods have become
notorious. Suspected subversives were brought into a room
where the seats were covered with cotton. Because of the tem-
perature of the room or stressful questioning, the victim was

made to sweat, and the cotton absorbed the perspiration. The fabric was then kept in a vault in a marked glass container for specially trained dogs to sniff if the suspect needed to be found later. The Stasi also perfected the hidden camera. They miniaturized it and placed it in cigarette containers and on clothing. These cameras saw everything.

During the Stasi's final days in 1990, after the fall of the wall, officials tried to shred their files. When shredders broke down from overuse, the workers tore the files by hand. Unfortunately for them, they stored the shreds in bags that were later confiscated by the new German government, and the long process of reassembling the documents started. In six years, three dozen workers went through only 300 bags. Later, computer-assisted data recovery helped get through 16,000 more bags, containing over 33 million pages. The files are being slowly opened to the public, and people have begun to know who had been spying on them. The shock felt by people betrayed by family and friends is rippling through German society even today.

THE FREE GERMAN YOUTH

As a teenager, Angela joined the Free German Youth (in German, the FDJ for Freie Deutsche Jugend). Most young people did. The organization was intended to teach socialist thought—food, shelter, and wealth should be distributed to each according to what they needed, and taken from each according to what they had. The group was more important than the individual. Freedom was less important than social order. Socialism tended to be less well defined than communism, but generally a socialist government had less control over its citizens than a communist one. Only slightly less, however. Socialist East Germany was in practice Communist East Germany to its citizens.

The FDJ had been formed in 1936 to oppose Adolph Hitler's Nazi Party, to promote socialist and communist principles against Hitler's fascist principles. In fascism, a leader takes control of the legislative and judicial branches of government and concentrates as much power in the executive branch as possible. Private business interests are protected by a fascist leader. Socialist and communist leaders do not usually try to protect private business. Instead, they try to bring the businesses under government control. Socialist and communist principles are different from fascist ones. In theory, they are natural enemies. Fascist governments often take power because wealthy and middle-class citizens are afraid of communists taking over a country, and figure a strong leader who keeps order is better than mob rule.

After Hitler's Germany was defeated in World War II in 1945, the FDJ became a powerful and important organization in East Germany. It was everywhere. The group provided more than roundtable meetings. It organized outings to lakes and parks, and even had dances. It ran its own travel agency to help organize trips for young people. It was a way for young people to feel part of a very large club, and Angela seemed to have enjoyed her time as a member. She read the official newspaper, the *Junge Welt*, which at one time had one of the largest circulations of any newspaper in the country. Some say she later became an officer in the FDJ, a secretary for "agitation and propaganda." Merkel has denied this—it is not a position she cares to talk about now. She says she simply organized social events and bought theater tickets. In any case, most agree she must have been enthusiastic about the FDJ and its mission. Her position there also shows that even though people perceive Angela to have been uninterested in politics until after the fall of the Berlin wall, she clearly liked to join others in a collective effort. She was a natural to rise in any organization she joined.

The pressures from the government were such, that if a young East German did not join the Free German Youth, she or he risked losing the opportunity to pursue a higher education. Angela was such a good student from a very early age, she must have known that she wanted to be on the difficult path of going to a university. Being the daughter of a pastor was an obstacle in that path, but her father's connections to the East German officials must have been strong enough to remove that obstacle. Though not able to become a teacher, she would at least be able to further her education.

BECOMING HIGHLY EDUCATED

During Angela's time, German schools had for many years been among the world's best. For the lower grade levels, students stayed in classrooms while teachers moved from class to class. Students sat at large tables, not desks. Exams tended to be essay-based and not multiple choice. Teachers were quite strict, and appointed for life after a certain trial period.

In high school, Angela became involved in an incident that reporters now use as an example of her political skills. One of her high school classes was led by a very unpopular teacher, who wanted to punish the entire class when some students did a group presentation somewhat different from what the teacher told them to do. They all could have been expelled from school, a very serious matter. Angela wrote a petition that she presented to some GDR officials whom her father and mother knew, explaining the situation. As a result, Angela's teacher was disciplined, not the students. Her class was saved.

In Germany, grades are usually given according to a one-through-six system, with a "1" being the equivalent of an "A-plus" in the United States, and a "6" the equivalent of an "F." Angela's grade point average was near a perfect 1. Only a small minority of German students qualify for a full university education (about 5 percent), and Angela was among that group. She had also been to several academic competitions, including one in Moscow to exhibit her skills in Russian. She bought her first record there, the Beatles' "Yellow Submarine." Listening to rock music was discouraged in East Germany, as was wearing blue jeans. There was enough of a rebel in Angela that she did both. The blue jeans she wore were gifts from relatives in

Angela Kasner *(front row, center)* poses in 1971 with her colleagues from the Mathematics Olympiad. Angela was skilled in mathematics and science and was an excellent student.

West Germany—most East Germans could not afford jeans. Her father had been very strict with her and her siblings. As a teenager, she found ways to be herself without getting into too much trouble with her father.

Universities in Germany are part of the free state education system. Students pay no tuition (although that may soon change). They do pay for books and room and board (universities there don't have dorms, so students share apartments). There are no fixed classes of students who study together and graduate together. University students choose their own program of study. Each student decides for himself or herself when to take final exams, and so some students spend as many as 10 years getting their college degree. The degree is called a "diplom" in the sciences and a "magister" in the arts. It is roughly equivalent to a master's degree in the United States.

In the fall of 1973, Angela left her home in Templin, and entered the University of Leipzig, which was also called Karl Marx University when she enrolled. It is one of the oldest universities in Europe, founded in 1409. Astronomer Tycho Brahe was a graduate, as was philosopher Friedrich Nietzsche. Today it has over 29,000 students. Angela concentrated on physics and physical chemistry, and was a brilliant student. She graduated from Karl Marx University in 1978 and decided to continue her education.

Only a small minority of university students go on to get their Ph.D., and Angela was one of them. She entered the Central Institute for Physical Chemistry of the Academy of Sciences in Berlin in 1978. Doctoral candidates in Germany take no formal classes, but do independent research under the guidance of a professor. They usually study, teach, and do research. They are paid a good salary, especially by East German standards. Angela wrote a Ph.D. dissertation called "The Calculations of Speed Constants of Elementary Reactions in Simple Carbohydrates." The study of simple carbohydrates was an especially important topic in the 1980s,

While camping with friends in Himmelpfort, East Germany, in 1973, Angela Kasner cooks up the evening meal. Not long after, Angela left home to attend Karl Marx University.

since the molecules' roles as primary energy sources in food were becoming more fully understood. Understanding reactions of simple carbohydrates is a key to understanding how people metabolize basic foods such as pasta, bread, and rice. Merkel contributed in some way to this understanding. She received her Ph.D. in 1986. She was now part of an elite group of highly educated East Germans.

LOVE AND MARRIAGE AND DIVORCE

Angela was not just a serious student. She enjoyed parties in both college and graduate school. She also took a part-time job waiting tables at a bar in Leipzig when she lived there. Her parents were providing her with about 250 marks per month (about $150), and she could earn more than 100 marks per month as a part-time waitress. That paid her rent. She was away from her father's restrictions for the first time, and she must have felt a personal freedom as never before.

While at the University of Leipzig, she met a man she would soon marry. He was also a student, named Ulrich Merkel, and he was a year older. They had a rapid courtship, and they married in 1977 when she was 23 and he 24. They rented a one-room apartment in Leipzig. They enjoyed the life of poor but happy students.

They moved to East Berlin when Merkel began her graduate studies at the Central Institute. They could afford only a run-down apartment with no hot water and no toilet. Life under socialist rule made finding good housing a nearly impossible undertaking. Ulrich was handy with tools, and he began to make repairs to the apartment as his wife studied and worked toward her doctorate. She has been very reluctant to discuss what happened then, but does say, "We got married because everyone got married. It sounds stupid, but I didn't go into the marriage with the necessary amount of seriousness." The marriage was not strong enough to survive the poor living conditions and emerging career differences. She left her husband in 1981; their divorce became final in 1982. She kept his last name, and the washing machine, and moved nearby into a barely furnished room. Her father later visited the room and wondered why she couldn't do better. Clearly, he disapproved.

At the Central Institute, Merkel studied and worked as a researcher. She eventually earned about 650 marks per month, and by all reports was a happily single woman living in East Berlin. She loved to go dancing, wear her blue jeans, listen to rock music, and immerse herself in her work. She enjoyed a happy and balanced life, and dated several men. Then, sometime in the mid-1980s after her divorce, she began dating her mentor, Professor Joachim Sauer. They both loved music, hiking, and long walks. They were both brilliant scientists. She loved being around friends more than he did, but their relationship deepened as time went on. Eventually, they began to live together.

In 1986, Merkel received permission to go to a cousin's wedding in Hamburg. It was her first trip back to the West since she was a baby. She was delighted by the West German intercity high-speed train, a new technological marvel she had never seen before. The speed and smoothness of the trip were unlike any train rides in East Germany. She was horrified when some West German students put their feet on the seats of the beautiful train. In East Germany, such behavior would never be allowed. She loved what she saw of West Germany, and began to think that Western democracy was a better system of government than what she had heard. Any part of the world that had such technological marvels as a high-speed train could not be all bad, despite what East Germans were taught.

Her personal life was very important to her. She went to a sauna every week, talked to her mother often, and had several friends. She loved her job, and was good at it. Her life was good, and it was peaceful. Only when the Berlin wall fell did her life change instantly and dramatically.

3

Political Awakening

WHEN THE BERLIN WALL WAS FINALLY BREACHED ON NOVEMBER 9, 1989, Merkel walked into West Berlin on that extraordinary night and changed her life. The sudden swirling events also changed her. The fall had not happened overnight, however. It was the result partly of a civil rights struggle now called "the peaceful revolution." The revolution of overthrowing the GDR had begun in the summer of 1989 with thousands of protesters and freedom marchers in Leipzig. They chanted "We are the people." When Soviet leader and reformer Mikhail Gorbachev visited East Germany in October 1989, he asked for reforms allowing more freedom. Long-time East German leader Erich Honecker was opposed to reforms. In fact, he was considering cracking down forcefully on all protesters. History, however, was moving against him. Honecker was forced to resign on October 19, 1989, since he did not have Gorbachev's support—

SHE KNEW HOW POWERFUL GOVERNMENT COULD BE, AND GETTING OUT FROM UNDER IT SEEMED TO LIBERATE HER IN EVERY WAY.

a necessary element needed for East Germany to maintain its restrictive policies.

The wall fell soon after. The unthinkable only a year before—a united Germany—became a realistic goal. On January 15, 1990, over 150,000 East Germans gathered in Leipzig and chanted "We are one people," instead of "We are the people." One word made all the difference.

A REUNITED GERMANY

One of the first things Merkel did after the "happiest night" of 11/9 was to join a group called the Democratic Awakening (Demokratischer Aufbruch), or DA. Her newly discovered political instincts now became the organizing force in her life. She knew how powerful government could be, and getting out from under it seemed to liberate her in every way. She wanted to take charge of those same forces that had dominated her life. The DA was a political movement founded by several East German church leaders to support a rapid unification with West Germany. The DA and other civil rights movements became much larger and more influential after the fall of the wall. Some of the members of DA were well known to the Kasners, including a charismatic leader named Lothar de Maizière. Partly as a result of her family contacts, Merkel immediately rose to become the DA spokeswoman to the press. Her intelligence and problem-solving skills were obvious, and she handled the media well, answering questions clearly and forcefully. She overcame her natural shyness quickly. She found a new confidence in her abilities. She had become empowered.

The DA did what many German political parties do: it went in search of other parties to form an alliance. Unlike American political parties that fight to keep their name recognition and remain independent, German politics forces coalitions and alliances between parties to gain political strength. The German political system is a parliamentary one, where not just individuals win political office—parties do as well. To rule in Parliament, a party must control more than 50 percent of the seats. To get that majority, the parties have to form coalitions with other parties.

The DA joined the Alliance for Germany in February 1990. The other parties in the alliance were the Christian Democratic Union (CDU) and the German Social Union. The alliance got the majority of seats in the first and only East German democratic elections (elections were held the March after the fall of the wall). Lothar de Maizière was made the new minister-president. Merkel was in the right place at the right time. She also made her own luck. She reportedly contacted de Maizière and told him how lucky the Alliance for Germany was to have the dedicated members of the DA. She made it known she was interested in a job in the new government. As a result, she was made the chief spokeswoman. She had gone from very private citizen to very public figure in a matter of a few months. She was definitely on the fast track.

Meanwhile, some 117,000 East Germans had left the country for good in the early days of 1990. The mandate of the new East German government headed by de Maizière, therefore, was to get rid of itself. It had to reunite with West Germany. Rarely in world history has a government been elected to destroy itself. As one commentator at the time said, Poland would remain Poland if communism there fell, but without communism there was no reason for East Germany to exist. Under Prime Minister de Maizière, East Germany negotiated

Months after the fall of the Berlin wall, allowing travel between East and West Germany, the two nations united as one. On March 30, 1990, West German Interior Minister Wolfgang Schauble *(left)* and East German chief negotiator Günther Krause *(right)* signed the Germany unification treaty in East Berlin.

the conditions of its death with West Germany. West German chancellor Helmut Kohl in turn reassured Britain and France that a reunited Germany would be no threat to them. World War II was still in the memories of the older world leaders, and a united Germany was still feared in some circles. Historians note that the United States and then-president

George H.W. Bush helped reunification by supporting it publicly and working for it with private diplomacy.

On October 3, 1990, Germany was officially reunified when the six federal states belonging to the former East Germany (Brandenburg, Berlin, Mecklenburg–West Pomerania, Saxony, Saxony-Anhalt, and Thuringia) formally joined the Federal Republic of Germany (West Germany). The existing West German constitution was used as the new constitution for the whole country. Later, that decision would make some of the former East Germans feel that they had not been reunited, but taken over. But, for the moment, all of Germany celebrated.

TRAFFIC LIGHT POLITICS

Students watching German elections and politics need a scorecard. Since a party cannot rule Parliament until it has more than 50 percent of the seats, coalitions of parties are a way of life. The main political parties are the Social Democratic Party (SPD), the Christian Democratic Union (CDU), the Christian Social Union (CSU), the Free Democratic Party (FDP), the Greens (usually allied with the SPD), and the Left Party (a relatively new party, mostly made up of SPD members who felt their party wasn't liberal enough). There are other parties, but unless one receives more than 5 percent of the votes in a general election, it is not represented in Parliament.

Each party has a color associated with it. The liberal SPD is red. The CDU and CSU have black as their symbolic color. The FDP is yellow, and the Greens are, naturally, green. So, "traffic light" coalitions of red, green, and yellow are possible when the SPD, FDP, and Greens get together and form a majority in Parliament. If the CDU, the FDP, and the Greens form a coalition, it will be the Jamaica coalition (the flag of Jamaica is black, yellow, and green). The coalition of red and black can be called a roulette coalition, because of the black and red slots in a roulette wheel. The country is certainly gambling when these parties get together. Whichever coalition is in power, it is usually a very colorful affair.

Political scientists like to point out the strengths and weaknesses of a parliamentary and coalition system. It is easier to pass legislation, since there is not as much opposing power as in a complete checks-and-balances system such as in the United States. A coalition system can be confusing, however, and no clear leader emerges directly from an election. Parties are elected, coalitions are formed, and deals need to be made to appoint a leader.

ELECTED TO OFFICE: 1990

The first general elections in the newly reunited Germany took place in December 1990. Merkel was a strong candidate for the new unified German Parliament. Her visibility as a spokeswoman for the now disbanded East German government had helped people get to know her, much like a presidential press secretary in the United States gets to be known in a short period of time.

She had chosen to become a member of the Christian Democratic Union. (Her old party, the DA, had disbanded, and been absorbed into the CDU in August 1990. DA Party leader de Maizière had been exposed as a former Stasi spy. The party didn't last long afterward.) Merkel's critics point out that she was late to join the DA, but very fast to leave it when she thought the CDU was more powerful. West German chancellor Kohl had thrown his support behind the East German CDU, and Merkel had quickly realized what that meant—she joined the CDU immediately. Her boss, friend, and roommate, Joachim Sauer, had chosen to join the more liberal SPD. She could not, and later said, "They sang such funny songs, like 'brothers, towards the sun, towards liberty.' I wanted to help with reconstruction."

Historians have noted that Merkel at this point in her life often talked about "reconstruction" and not "reunification."

She knew that the hard work was not just in getting the Germanies back together, but also making their economies work together. East Germany lagged behind West Germany in factory modernization, roads, housing, schools, and every other sector in the economy. The former East Germany would need to be rebuilt, and someone had to pay for it. The central-planned economy that led to economic stagnation would have to be replaced by a free market system. Capitalism was needed, and Merkel was a believer in capitalism. She seemed to be one step ahead of many others in her planning.

Merkel ran on a platform of solving the problems of modernization and reconstruction with investment and free market economics. She was successful, beating two West Germans. She was elected as a CDU member to the house of Parliament known as the *Bundestag*. She immediately began to attract attention since she was a woman and a former East German. Kohl knew his place in history would be decided by how smoothly the German reunification took place, and he knew that one way to ensure a smooth transition was to give recognition to "Ossies," as the East Germans are called (West Germans are "Wessies"). He had become popular in the former East German states because he made the East German currency, the Ostmark, equal in value to the West German Deutschmark. As a result, the former East Germans did not have their savings destroyed.

Kohl also was famous for wanting those around him to hold similar views to his own. He must have felt he could easily influence this new young politician and that she would do what he wanted her to do. He would be proved wrong.

THE FEDERAL MINISTER FOR WOMEN AND YOUTH

Kohl personally chose Merkel for his cabinet in 1991. She became the Federal Minister for Women and Youth. The ministry had originally been the Federal Ministry for Family Affairs. It was changed in 1969 to the Federal Ministry for

Angela Merkel speaks on the phone at CDU party headquarters in Berlin in 1990. Critics have asserted that Merkel's party alliances changed to accommodate her rise to power, but Merkel says she was motivated by the desire to help her country during the difficult reconstruction period.

Youth, Family, and Health. The health portion of the organization became larger and larger, so when Merkel took over
the job a new ministry had been created, the Federal Ministry
for Health. She took over the cabinet position overseeing the
issues of women and young people. At 36, she was the youngest
minister in German postwar history. Even though some journalists continued to make fun of her appearance—she wore
no makeup and favored frumpy clothes and flat sandals—she
slowly won people over through her sheer hard work. She never
seemed to get tired.

Reporters at the time noted that she was an effective
administrator, now responsible for a great number of people
and for the first time running a large organization. She had
always been a good listener, and able to find compromises
that worked. She did so again. She started or continued several special projects, including studying family-friendly work
practices such as part-time employment and job-sharing. The
ministry managed grants to increase educational opportunities for women and university-age students. Special doctoral
grants for women, intended to increase the number of female
professors are also still part of the ministry's mission. Training
for disabled women and young people is a vital component of
the mission of the ministry.

Her reputation as a rising political figure began to spread.
Only a few months after taking over as Federal Minister for
Women and Youth, her party called again. The CDU needed
a deputy or vice chairperson. Kohl told a CDU party meeting
in Dresden in December 1991 that Merkel represented three
groups the CDU needed to pay more attention to—former
East Germans (Ossies), women, and young people. She was 37
at the time, and very young compared to most of the leaders
in the CDU. Merkel took yet another step upward when she
won 86.4 percent of the vote for deputy chair. She seemed to
have stepped into a party leadership vacuum, and she filled it.

She was now a force within the CDU party itself, one of its top officials, as well as a cabinet-level administrator.

MINISTER FOR THE ENVIRONMENT AND REACTOR SAFETY

In 1994, Kohl appointed Merkel to another ministry, overseeing the environment and reactor safety. Her background in physics made her particularly suited for this more visible and highly controversial post. Kohl had taken to calling Merkel "das Mädchen" ("the girl") since she was his youngest cabinet minister. He felt she was ready to take on the challenges posed by both the Greens, the political party devoted to environmental causes, and the nuclear industry. The issue of nuclear power would become the biggest challenge to her political career now and for years to come.

Like many countries, Germany had believed that building nuclear power plants was a good way to solve a growing energy crisis intensified by the oil shortages in the early 1970s. Nuclear plants have several advantages: unlike coal-fired plants, they don't emit air pollution and so don't increase global warming if they are working properly; and they don't usually pollute water, unlike some other methods of generating electricity; and they don't disrupt the land, as dam building does. Some experts in the 1960s and 1970s thought that most of the world's electricity would come from nuclear power plants by the year 2000. That prediction did not come true.

The disadvantages of nuclear power plants can be summed up in two events. The first was on March 29, 1979. The number 2 reactor at the Three Mile Island nuclear power plant near Harrisburg, Pennsylvania, lost its coolant water and about 50 percent of the reactor core melted. The cause was both mechanical failure and human operator failure. The result was that unknown amounts of radioactive materials escaped into the air. Cleanup and payment of damages cost over a billion dollars, which is more than the reactor cost to build.

The second event took place on April 26, 1986. A series of explosions in one of the reactors in a nuclear power plant in the Chernobyl region of the Ukraine (then a part of the Soviet Union) blew the roof off the building, throwing radioactive debris and dust high into the atmosphere. Tens of thousands of people were exposed to dangerous levels of radioactivity. No mention was made of the disaster until Swedish scientists detected massive amounts of radioactivity in their skies, and the Soviets confessed what they knew about the Chernobyl accident. Poor reactor design and poor training of a cleaning crew were responsible for the explosions. Greenpeace estimates that the total death count from the accident may be as high as 32,000 people. The official death toll is 3,576. Higher than normal rates of cancers, thyroid tumors, and cataracts continue to plague the people living near the area.

Even though the two highly visible accidents brought new reactor construction almost to a halt in America and Europe, another problem may be just as serious as the risk of an accident. All nuclear power plants produce radioactive nuclear waste when their cores wear out, and no one really knows how to dispose of high-level radioactive waste properly. The waste must be stored for thousands of years. Most countries favor the strategy of burying the waste deep underground, in salt, granite, or clay formations. Germany has chosen a site in the town of Gorleben, and nuclear waste comes there from power plants all over Germany to be stored in above-ground warehouses. Later, if approved, the waste will be buried deep underground in a salt dome at the edge of the town.

The radioactive waste arrives at Gorleben in large steel-lined boxes called castors, carried on a train or truck. Armed with evidence that the steel-lined boxes themselves were leaking radiation, protesters from various German environmental groups tried to block the shipments to Gorleben in 1995. They disrupted roads by sitting down, placing tractors with flat tires as blockades, and setting fire to bales of straw. Merkel had to

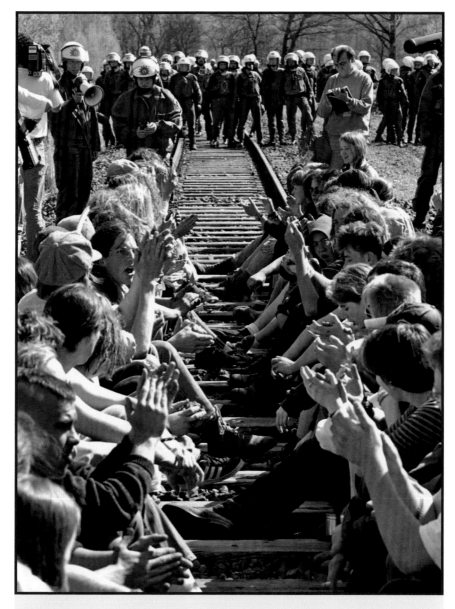

Educated as a scientist, Angela Merkel held the position of Minister for the Environment and Reactor Safety, a post that increased her profile and challenged her political skills. Germany's use of nuclear power is controversial among its citizens, and in 1995, demonstrators attempted to block the railway used to convey nuclear waste to the town of Gorleben.

be the one who called out record numbers of police to guard the shipments. The officers used water cannons, helicopters, and police dogs to move thousands of demonstrators out of the way. Many Germans were shocked at the sight of such violence against their own citizens. Merkel was then portrayed as being the defender of a suddenly unpopular German nuclear industry, and not caring enough about the people exposed to radiation from the containers. Many groups called for her resignation. She faced her first political crisis.

She survived the crisis by staying calm, listening to the evidence on all sides, and appealing to rationality and not emotions. No one could prove a health crisis really existed. The courts had already said the shipments could go through. She rode out the storm. She had learned another valuable political lesson—remain calm and keep reassuring people that their worst fears are not based in real evidence and in science. Her critics say she was too sympathetic to the nuclear power interests and did not protect the German people living near the transportation routes of the radioactive waste. She had Kohl's unwavering support, however. He must have been glad he was not the one directly drawing the wrath of the environmentalists and most of the German media.

THE NUCLEAR ENERGY ISSUE

The world is deeply divided on the issue of nuclear power. Virtual moratoriums on nuclear power plant construction have been in effect for years in the United States, Germany, Italy, Finland, and the Netherlands, but reactors have been just completed or are under construction in India, Taiwan, South Korea, Brazil, China, and Argentina. France gets 78 percent of its electricity from nuclear plants, and China gets less than 2 percent. Several industrialized countries currently get 30 percent or more of their electricity from nuclear plants: France, Belgium, Bulgaria, Hungary, Japan, Lithuania,

Slovakia, South Korea, Sweden, Switzerland, Slovenia, and Ukraine. France, for example, felt the oil shocks of 1973-74 acutely, and with few energy resources of its own but a great deal of heavy engineering experience, it embraced nuclear energy as no other country has.

Energy experts have come up with at least two very different scenarios for the world's use of nuclear energy:

- **Scenario 1:** The world will decrease from the current 15 percent of electricity being generated by nuclear power to 11 percent or lower by the year 2015. The famous accident at the Chernobyl plant in Russia in April 1986 will continue to cast a deadly pall over citizens, politicians, and utility companies, all of whom are afraid of the costs of any more nuclear accidents. Demand for electricity will not rise as fast as most predictions, and solar and wind technology will develop more rapidly than has been the case. Fossil-fuel prices will not rise enough to make nuclear power even more economical. Low-emission technology will not be required in fossil-fuel-burning power plants. Nuclear waste sites will continue to be a source of tremendous tension in possibly affected communities. Delays such as those at Nevada's Yucca Mountain in the United States and Gorleben in Germany will continue.

- **Scenario 2:** The world will increase from the current 15 percent to 19 percent or more by 2015. The need for electricity, especially in developing countries, will continue to grow at a pace that forces more nuclear power capability. The World Economic Council's estimate that global consumption of electricity will grow by at least 50 percent in the next 20 years will prove correct. Advanced designs in nuclear power plants make the public less afraid of nuclear accidents. Plants will become more efficient, require less nuclear fuel, and have shorter construction times. No major accidents will be reported as new and old plants are run more efficiently by people who know how to run them. The nuclear waste problem will have been solved to at least a workable degree.

No one knows which scenario will be closer to reality in 2015. The debate about nuclear power rages on, and Merkel will likely be near the center of it in Europe.

MORE ENVIRONMENTAL POLITICS

Nuclear power was not the only environmental issue in which Merkel became embroiled. A major German environmental organization (equivalent to America's Sierra Club) called the German Union for Nature Preservation accused Merkel and the Kohl government of listening more to business interests than environmental advocates on many issues. The group called Merkel's attempts to lower greenhouse gas emissions vague and inadequate. They noted in a 1996 report that she did not push initiatives for cleaner running cars. The United States passed Germany in 1996 in sales of recycling and solid waste management technology, a field Germany had dominated for many years.

Supporters of Merkel's environmental policies defend her by saying that under her administration, the former East German states dramatically improved their environmental record. Stricter regulations for air and water pollutants were put in place. Factories that used sulfur-rich brown coal started to switch to cleaner-burning black coal. Levels of mercury, copper, and arsenic in the environment dropped as Merkel's regulations took effect. She supported initiatives to have computer makers take back discarded terminals, disk drives, and printers. She encouraged manufacturers of household products to set up similar recycling programs.

Merkel also took the lead in asking the European Union (the EU, an alliance of several European countries) to tackle

SHE SHOWED A WILLINGNESS TO TACKLE PROBLEMS ON A LARGER SCALE THAN JUST COUNTRY-BY-COUNTRY.

environmental problems as a region. She said that the natural environment does not coincide with human borders. She suggested that a tax policy to cut emissions should be enacted on a regional basis, so no one country found its economy hurt by new restrictions. She showed a willingness to tackle problems on a larger scale than just country-by-country. It was a strategy that would define her leadership. She strengthened her emphasis on the relatively new field of environmental ethics. She published an article in the journal *Science* in July 1998 and expanded on her environmental principles:

> A common basic understanding of environmental ethics is needed to ensure that protection of the natural foundation of life becomes a major consideration in all political and individual action. . . . In the long term, "progress" works against us if it continues to be detrimental to nature. This realization will find increasing acceptance. Environmental protection will play a central role in the 21st century and will be a major challenge for politicians and scientists alike.

CUTTING TIES TO KOHL

The German elections of 1998 provided a shock to Kohl and his administration. Germans were becoming tired of high unemployment rates and slow progress in bringing the former East German state economies up to the level of performance of the West German states. They elected a coalition government headed by Gerhard Schröder of the liberal SPD and the Green Party. After 16 years in office, Kohl's CDU was out. Merkel was suddenly no longer in the cabinet when Schröder installed his new ministers.

During this period in 1998 between jobs, Merkel took time to get married for the second time, to Dr. Joachim Sauer, whose fame as a physical chemist had consistently risen. They had been living together for many years, and as their relationship deepened, so did their commitment to each other. So, on December 30, 1998, they went to the Bonn Registry Office and legally married. Later the world would learn that Merkel's parents were not invited to any wedding ceremony and didn't find out about the wedding until the next day, New Year's Eve. While they were in the kitchen, Merkel mentioned to her mother that she had remarried. Some have said the wedding was a spur-of-the-moment decision, but others say it was planned and shows that she was no longer close to her parents. Because they had been living together for so many years, however, the marriage license itself may have seemed to them only a formality and not the occasion for a huge celebration.

Sauer became a professor of physical chemistry at Humboldt University in Berlin in 1993, and has authored more than 200 publications while giving over 220 invited lectures around the world. He had helped Merkel with her dissertation research, and had mentored her in physical chemistry before she received her Ph.D. He was, however, only five years older than she, so they were close enough in age to share many interests outside the laboratory, especially music and hiking. His last name means "sour" in German, and some of the German press have been annoyed that he seems to live up to his name. He always asks that they leave him alone. Like her first husband, he has no comment to make publicly.

Merkel soon took a new job within the CDU: She became its secretary-general. It was her responsibility to help CDU candidates get elected in their various states, called länder, and she was an immediate success. In 1999, she coordinated CDU victories in six out of seven provincial elections, breaking the hold of the SPD-Green coalition in the *Bundesrat,* the second house of the German Parliament (the Bundestag is the first). She was organized, hard-working, available, and effective. She had now proven that she could get people to vote again for the CDU.

In late 1999 and the early months of 2000, a scandal rocked Germany. Kohl and several other heads of the CDU admitted they had received illegal campaign contributions and put the money in Swiss banks. German candidates are allowed to receive campaign contributions, but there are many restrictions on them. Most of their campaign money comes from public funds, so candidates are not in debt to corporations that donate money. All private contributions have to be recorded publicly, so corruption is infrequent in German politics. Kohl had not recorded all the contributions.

Reporters hounded Merkel and asked if she knew anything about the "slush funds." She denied knowing anything about the "financial shenanigans." While some other CDU leaders put loyalty to the party first and defended Kohl, Merkel tried to find out what really happened. When she became convinced Kohl was in the wrong she told the German press and public exactly what she thought. She wrote a newspaper article condemning Kohl. Some CDU party members were convinced she had betrayed her mentor, the man who had given her a flying start in national politics. They felt she had stabbed Kohl in the back. Merkel felt that Kohl had betrayed a trust, and should no longer be a leader of the party. She put her loyalty to truth ahead of loyalty to the party. Many Germans praised her honesty. If Kohl thought Merkel would always do what he wanted her to do, he now saw and felt her independence. She had outgrown her political father.

The CDU was now in crisis. With so much money drained from the party by the scandal, including a $21 million fine, the CDU was near bankruptcy. The ruling SPD-Green Party had moved to the political center and the CDU was losing its reason for being. It was the conservative, small-government, free-market party. As the SPD-Greens moved closer to that position, many thought the CDU would disappear. In Italy, the party had vanished. Many waited for its death in Germany as well.

PRESIDENT OF THE CDU

At a three-day party meeting in April 2000, the remains of the CDU gathered to regroup. For the first time since 1951, Kohl was not heard from. He did pick a successor, however. He wanted Wolfgang Schauble to take his place as head of the CDU. But the party looked to another person, the one who had shown honesty and courage and spoken out against Kohl. Merkel was elected president of the CDU on April 10, 2000. She was a surprise—the CDU had traditionally been a male-dominated Catholic group from West Germany. Merkel was a Protestant, a woman, and from the East. Many thought she was presiding over a dead body. Reports of its death proved to be premature.

When Kohl was the head of the CDU, banquets with roast duck, expensive smoked fish, and large tables full of exotic delicacies were standard. When Merkel took over, her cele-bratory dinner for the party elite was cold ham, potato salad, and cabbage. She knew the significance of details such as these, to show that the party was going to cut frills and man-age its budgets better. The party now cut expenses by having fewer publications, renting out part of the Berlin headquar-ters, and eliminating personnel. The messages coming out of party headquarters would be clear and concise. The new leader would be more available to the press. Reporter Roger Cohen of the *New York Times* asked CDU member Hannelore Heuser what he thought of the changes. Heuser replied, "To me, Ms. Merkel is about a new style in politics, one that is honest, direct, and clear. That is the most drastic and sig-nificant change after what we now perceive as the dangerous murkiness of the Kohl system."

Angela Merkel poses for the press on April 10, 2000, shortly after being elected president of the CDU. As a woman, a Protestant, and an East German, Merkel did not embody traditional party leadership.

Soon after she was elected president of the party, Merkel granted an extensive interview to Stefan Theil of *Newsweek*. She began to outline her new party message by looking at her own past.

The slogan we used in the 1998 election was "Security instead of risk." In my opinion, we should turn that around to "Risk instead of security." The world is changing rapidly, and we have to have the courage to see change as something positive instead of being as frightened by change as many

Germans still are today. In East Germany in 1989, we faced the necessity of total and radical change. Instead of letting ourselves be paralyzed by the risks, we decided to make the best of it, and it brought us a lot of good.

Merkel went on to tell Theil that the CDU stood for less bureaucracy and more trust in the workings of a free market. Competition, not government, would decide which companies prosper and which fail. When she was asked what the "Christian" portion of the Christian Democratic Union meant in a Germany where the church was declining, she replied:

> I think the "C" [in CDU] stands for giving people a compass of values. We live in a world today where we can go anywhere we want via the Internet. Giving people a sense of their roots and values is something where a Christian viewpoint can be a great help. The "C" also stands for seeing that all humans have failings, including politicians. I lived in a dictatorship where a group of people thought they were historically determined to rule over others. A Christian viewpoint rules that out.

A Major Setback: 2002

Merkel's rise in the party had been fast and furious. When the general elections came in 2002, Merkel and many others expected her to become the CDU nominee for chancellor to run against Schröder. Instead, she suffered her first major political setback.

The CDU had a sister party, the Christian Social Union (CSU), which was concentrated in Bavaria. The CDU and CSU could always be counted on to be for and against the same policies. In the federal elections of 2002, most observers assumed that the close history of the parties would continue, and the head of the CDU would become the CDU-CSU candidate for chancellor. Instead, the head of the CSU, Edmund Stoiber, decided to challenge Merkel for the right to run against Schröder's SPD-Green government. Suddenly, not having a regional power base and a network of old friends worked against Merkel. Many big business interests reportedly supported Stoiber over Merkel, and some felt the prejudice against an East German woman finally came into play. Others said Merkel's lack of glamour and charisma worked against her. The camera did not seem to love her. Still others say Merkel decided to avoid a showdown within her party and gracefully let the older Stoiber take the candidacy. She knew she had risen very far very fast and had not paid all the dues a politician must pay. She knew some senior members were against her. She knew she threatened the old guard.

Stoiber won the right to become the CDU-CSU candidate, and to oppose Schröder. The final election was close, but Stoiber proved to be an ineffective campaigner and lost his early lead in the polls. Schröder defeated Stoiber, or rather the SPD-Green Party defeated the CDU-CSU, and Schröder was re-elected. Schröder was not especially popular, since unemployment was high and he had cut unemployment benefits. As a result, consumer spending in Germany was down. But, the German people felt he needed more time to stimulate the economy. As a rule, German voters did not like to change governments often. And they had not warmed up to Stoiber.

The CDU had learned a lesson. It would not overlook its new star again. She had not provoked a fight within the party and had given way when Stoiber won the candidacy. The party members would not forget her ability to work within the party. She would soon be their candidate for chancellor.

4

Becoming the German Leader

THE CDU WAS STUNG BY LOSING TO THE OPPOSITION PARTY, AND NOW turned to Merkel to find a way to win in the next federal election. Even the senior members of the party realized the CDU needed a change and that they should not stand in Merkel's way any longer. She went back to work with a vengeance. In February 2003, the CDU picked up ground and won several regional elections, putting the party back in control of one of the two houses of Parliament, the Bundesrat. Over the next two years, she continued to build support at the local level for her party, and do all the small things that a party must do to regain office. Her efforts paid off: On May 22, 2005, the CDU won local elections in German states they had not led for almost 40 years.

Chancellor Schröder decided then that enough was enough. He believed he could beat the "gray mouse" (another common description of Merkel, along with "the girl") in a general election. So, he took the unusual step of announcing that the national elections held normally in 2006 would be held instead in September 2005 (German political rules allow this). Like many people, he had underestimated the young, unglamorous woman from a small town far away. Some in his party were stunned, but knew Schröder was a master campaigner and an expert in using televised debates to his advantage.

THE CANDIDATE: MAY 30, 2005

The CDU leadership was surprised at the announcement of an early general election. They needed to move fast. The party made it official on May 30, 2005: Angela Merkel would be their candidate in September to run against Schröder and the SPD-Green parties. She was the first woman ever chosen to be a candidate for chancellor.

CDU staff members packed into the balconies of the party headquarters in Berlin and began a night of tributes and celebration. The leader of the Christian Social Union, Edmund Stoiber, stepped to the podium to make the announcement. He had defeated Merkel three years earlier and was opposed to her emphasis on the level of change needed in German government. He now had to give her his blessing: "Angela Merkel has the full confidence of the Christian Democrats and the Christian Social Union." When she approached the lectern to accept the party nomination, Merkel heard chants of "Angie, Angie" from the balconies. She was in tears by the time she spoke.

She thanked her supporters and her party, but then got down to business. She didn't believe in long-winded speeches. She began to list the issues that her country faces.

> The lowest economic growth of all 25 member states of the European Union, debts as high as never before in the history of the Federal Republic of Germany, people fearing for their pensions, a dramatic increase of poverty in our country, the feeling of two-class health care, but above all the depressing number of 5 million registered unemployed.

German chancellor Gerhard Schröder *(above)*, who held the office from 1998-2004, lost favor among German citizens due to his reform program, which included cuts to welfare and other programs. With his party weakened, the time was right for Merkel and the CDU to take control of the country's government.

Merkel went on to catalog more of the economic problems that voters originally elected the Schröder-led government to solve. Liberal parties tend to concentrate more on putting people back to work than conservative parties do, and the SPD-Green coalition had said in 2002 that it would strengthen the economy and decrease unemployment. Merkel was showing they had not done what the voters elected them to do, without quite saying what her party would do that was different. She was too smart to get specific this early in the campaign. That was for later.

National Public Radio's Emily Harris covered the speech for an American audience, and interviewed citizens in the streets of Berlin and Cologne to see what they thought. Teacher Edith Coverlink said, "She's not funny. Not at all. And she doesn't seem to be a very feminine person. But I think it isn't necessary for a woman to be very charming. It's necessary to have the possibility to be a good politician." Coverlink was not sure, but she was thinking of voting for Merkel. One man called her a "clown," apparently in reference to her haircut. Another said, "She doesn't have a chance." Harris went to a performance by a comedian named Reiner Kronert, who specializes in making fun of German politicians. For his Merkel skit, he went behind a curtain and came out with a large blonde bowl-cut wig. He hunched his shoulders and frowned. He looked grim and scolding. Everyone knew who he was making fun of. He later told Harris that people used to simply laugh at his act; now, they want to hear more about her. She had captured their interest.

THE CAMPAIGN TRAIL: SUMMER 2005

The scene became a common one throughout the summer of 2005 in German cities and towns. Police revved their motorcycles. Supporters waved huge banners. Mick Jagger's recorded voice boomed out of loudspeakers looming over the crowds: "Oh Angie, Oh Angie, when will those clouds all disappear? Angie, Angie, where will it lead from here?" The candidate stood and looked a bit unsure of how to react at first. Then, she raised her arms straight up, reached for the sky, and beamed at the crowd. The "Angie" banners waved furiously. She then delivered a very serious talk on the problems of the country. She wagged her finger like a stern headmistress, and sometimes stumbled with her words out of sheer fatigue. She

She knew that many people thought of her as a scientific cold fish, but she was always honest and straightforward.

seemed a little old-fashioned when she talked about her desire to serve her country with hard work. She didn't tell cute little stories, or have a handy joke fitted for the town she was in. She got into a bit too much detail on problems and how to fix them. A few people began to wander away. Then, she finished her speech. The recording of Mick Jagger started to play again: "All the dreams we held so close seemed to all go up in smoke." The crowds went home, knowing just a bit more about this no-nonsense politician; some were now converts to her seriousness, some turned off by it.

Political advisers suggested the candidate get a makeover. In the middle of the summer, Merkel now appeared with a new haircut, with layers and highlights. She then had makeup professionally applied. Merkel had said before the campaign that "If all people have to worry about is the way I look then their lives must be very fortunate." She adjusted her view of how important appearances are when running for national office. She kissed very few babies that summer, however. She hated that side of politicking. She knew that many people thought of her a scientific cold fish, but she was always honest and straightforward. She could and did soften her appearance for the cameras, but she was who she was.

Newspapers began to publish more pieces on Merkel, with many trying to show readers her private side. Some covered the garden at her weekend cottage in the village of Hoheswerde, where she and her husband liked to retreat for peace and quiet. They tended the asters, marigolds, and kohlrabi. Papers critical of Merkel noted that her husband did more work than she did

Merkel supporters hold up placards reading "Vote Change" and "Angie" during a rally in Osnabruck on August 30, 2005. It was obvious that Germans were looking for a change in leadership.

in the garden. Papers sympathetic to her covered their jogs, and their enjoyment of the music of Wagner at the annual Bayreuth festival. They covered her love of Dustin Hoffman movies, and cooking potato soup for her friends.

Some papers noted that her mother was a SPD member, not a CDU devotee. They claimed there was tension in the family. Papers reported rumors about her days in East Germany, and whether she had an unhappy childhood. Was her father too cold to her? Informants told the media that Merkel was seen standing in the doorway of her apartment on several

Parts of the campaign
did not go well at all for her.

occasions after her divorce from her first husband kissing different men goodbye. Why didn't she have children? Why wouldn't her husband talk to the media? Why aren't they together more, holding hands? The frenzy of a political campaign in any country leads to accusations and innuendos. When a woman is involved, the frenzy seems to be even more heightened. The personal and the political become inseparable.

Parts of the campaign did not go well at all for her. One of the CDU ministers suggested after a sensational child murder case that summer that killing babies was much more common in the former East Germany. That did not help Merkel's popularity with this crucial support base. Edmund Stoiber, the man who beat her for the CDU candidacy in 2002, suggested that former East Germans were not completely trustworthy and perhaps not intelligent enough to make the right voting choices. Now, some suspected that a few senior CDU officials were trying to sabotage Merkel. When Merkel finally faced Schröder in a televised debate and twice confused the terms "net" and "gross" income, some wondered if she had sabotaged herself. Experts in political campaigning say that sheer candidate fatigue plays a large role in any election season. Candidates push themselves to exhaustion, like boxers or marathon runners. When they are exhausted, they tend to make mistakes. Merkel was no exception.

THE CAMPAIGN ISSUES, 2005

The major issue in the 2005 German national election was the economy. After seven years of Schröder's SPD-Green coalition leadership, German unemployment was still high, at 11.6 percent nationally and over 25 percent in the former East German states. Merkel cleverly exploited the economic issue at first by saying Great Britain had a stronger economy that Germany. The rivalry between Germany and Great Britain over economic supremacy in Europe is an old one, and Merkel made the German voters very aware that they were losing to their old rival.

An aging population had pushed social security payments past what workers were contributing. As a result, the deficit was booming. Schröder had tried to cut unemployment benefits and social security payments, but this was very unpopular and not very effective. Merkel offered a solution to the booming deficits: raise the Value Added Tax (VAT) from 16 percent to 18 percent. The VAT is essentially a European sales tax, but is added to both goods and services. The sales taxes in the various U.S. states apply to goods only, not services, so the VAT is a much larger tax on many more things. As such, it is a very important source of revenue for European governments. For the more conservative party to suggest raising taxes in an American election would be a very unusual event. In Germany, the proposal showed that Merkel was prepared to take the political consequences of an unpopular, but effective, solution. Schröder attacked her plan unmercifully.

The second major issue of the campaign was the Iraq war, begun primarily by the United States in 2003 in an effort to overthrow the regime of Saddam Hussein. Schröder had been against the war from the beginning, as had a clear majority of the German voting public. He allied himself with France's strong and continual criticism of the Bush administration on the war. Merkel was one of the only European political figures to say publicly that the goals of the war were noble and correct. She said Germany had to stop bashing the United States, and that her administration would have friendlier relations with America and its foreign policies. She said she had grown up in a country without freedom, and knew more than most how precious it was. She supported America.

Angela Merkel and her husband, Joachim Sauer, attend the Bayreuth opera festival on July 25, 2003. Notoriously camera shy, Sauer has remained out of the spotlight during his wife's term in office. After the Bayreuth festival, he was nicknamed "The Phantom of the Opera" by the German press.

A final issue in the campaign was the role of government. Schröder, like Stoiber, believed that small changes to policy could bring Germany up to a new level of competitiveness in the global market. Government still had to be a strong regulator of businesses, a guide for scientific research, and a source of funding for many kinds of projects. Merkel believed that government needed to be smaller and to get out of the way of businesses. She sounded very much like a moderate Republican in the United States. She felt government should dramatically simplify taxes, even suggesting she would support a flat tax (all people pay the same percentage of their income as a tax) when she told reporters she wanted to appoint a flat tax proponent as her minister of economic policy. Again, Schröder attacked her flat tax ideas, saying only the rich would benefit.

Suddenly, Merkel was on the defensive, and the seven-year record of the Schröder government was not the main issue in the campaign. He spoke in generalities about his record, but was extremely specific in his attacks on her. Her personality became an issue. She was a problem-solver and got into great detail analyzing problems. She rarely smiled at voters. She replied harshly to hecklers, not hiding her annoyance with them. She did not tell simple stories with happy endings to appease her listeners. She had come a long way from East Germany, but she did not like to tell her story. She wanted to talk about the future.

As a result, Merkel's lead in the polls was cut to almost nothing. She clearly had to learn a lot about national election campaigning. Instead of being very vague and attacking her opponent, she was offering specific solutions to real problems. Even if media experts warn against such honesty in any national election, some of the German people seemed to like her honesty. Reporter Mark Landler wrote just before the election that he interviewed many people, and one seemed to sum up Merkel's supporters: Hanna Kaltenbach told him,

"She has so much courage. Schröder is a media star, but he is shallow."

THE ELECTION, 2005

Finally, election day came, on September 18. The polls and exit interviews after people had voted that morning showed only a very narrow lead for Merkel and the CDU. The tense hours of waiting as results came in were agonizing for both parties. Late that night, the results were in. The CDU-CSU had won 35.2 percent of the vote. Schröder's SPD-Green coalition won 34.2 percent. Both parties claimed victory since neither party had a majority in the Bundestag. Under German election rules, a coalition government would have to be set up reflecting the proportions of votes each party received. Any ruling coalition had to have more than 50 percent of the seats in the Bundestag. To get that many votes, a grand coalition of the CDU and the SPD was needed. Black and red would be joined in the roulette wheel of German politics. No other combination worked, even though both sides tried to avoid a grand coalition. That grand coalition would require days of negotiations to see who would hold what jobs. The negotiations were not easy and often not pleasant. Political rivals usually have strong feelings about their opponents after a long campaign. Merkel and Schröder were intense competitors. Direct negotiations between them would be difficult. The election was beginning to look like a mess.

After almost three weeks of backroom dealing, Merkel was declared the new chancellor on November 10. However, the SPD would hold 8 of the 15 cabinet seats. Many political scientists have stated that Merkel must have been a formidable negotiator during the time between the election and the compromise. All parties needed to officially approve the deal, and a vote in Parliament was taken. Merkel received a majority of the delegates' votes, 397 out of 614 votes cast, on November 22, 2005. Fifty-one members of the Grand Coalition voted against her, or abstained. Clearly, there were still some hard feelings.

CDU general secretary Volker Kauder presents Angela Merkel with congratulatory flowers, one day after she was elected to the chancellorship.

The speaker of Parliament, Norbert Lammert, announced after the vote: "Dear Mrs. Merkel, you are the first ever elected female head of government in Germany. That is a strong signal for many women and certainly for some men, too." Laughter rippled through the room. She was, at last, the head of Germany. The first person to greet her was Gerhard Schröder. He smiled broadly.

She still didn't have time for lobsters at the Kempinski with her mother. She had to swear-in her cabinet. She had five women and ten men to confirm; they would now become the various ministers who would help govern. Three of the ministers were already positioned from the SPD-Green government. She wanted the best ministers, and she knew their experience would be valuable. Her rival, Edmund Stoiber, was offered the post of minister for economics and technology. He withdrew his name. Merkel wanted to keep peace in her own party, but apparently Stoiber did not have the same goal.

After an exhausting campaign and weeks of tense negotiations, Merkel was not even able to take a little time to herself. Politicians often feel a great sense of accomplishment after a victory, but they also know that running for office is very different from holding office. Her days of holding one of the most powerful offices in Europe, and the world, were now just beginning. Friends who know her well said she would stay calm, keep her feet on the ground, and maybe make some potato soup.

5

A New World Leader

THE DAY AFTER SHE WAS SWORN IN AS CHANCELLOR, MERKEL BEGAN A whirlwind trip, demonstrating her energy and skill in making alliances. She got on a plane and went to Paris to meet with French president Jacques Chirac. It was more than a symbolic meeting. Some advisers had urged her to travel east and meet first with Poland and some of the Baltic states. Merkel knew, however, that history and tradition dictated certain protocols, and so she visited France first, to emphasize the importance of their relationship. Then she flew to Brussels to meet with European Union leaders. She also met with North Atlantic Treaty Organization (NATO) secretary-general Jaap de Hoop Scheffer. This was an important meeting. NATO is a security alliance among 26 countries. An attack on one country in NATO is an attack on all countries in NATO. The organization was formed in 1949 to protect western Europe from the Soviet Union. Despite the end of the Cold War, the alliance is

"I THINK GERMANY IS DESTINED, PARTLY AS A RESULT OF ITS GEOGRAPHIC POSITION, TO BE A MEDIATOR AND A BALANCING FACTOR."

—Angela Merkel

still important—NATO-led forces took over military operations in southern Afghanistan in July 2006, for example. From Brussels, Merkel went to London to meet with British Prime Minister Tony Blair. Reporters trying to keep up with her were exhausted.

When she returned home, she received her first state visitor, President Pohamba of Namibia. He visited Berlin for five days. Namibia and Germany have close ties because Namibia was a former German colony.

On November 30, 2005, Merkel gave her first major speech as chancellor. Her primary focus was Germany's role in the European Union (EU), a relatively new alliance of 25 European countries. Many of the members of the EU now have a common currency, the euro, managed by the European Central Bank. Decision-making within the EU is enormously complicated, with many issues to confront. France had refused to ratify the EU constitution only weeks before, and some called it a European crisis. A June 2005 summit meeting of the EU had been a disaster, with no agreement about its budget. Leaders wondered what role Germany intended to play. Merkel wasted no time in outlining a simple and practical EU agenda:

> I don't think it makes sense to go round and round in circles arguing about this crisis. We have to manage it instead. But that's something we can only do together with our neighbors, our partners, the big ones and the small ones. I think

Germany is destined, partly as a result of its geographic position, to be a mediator and a balancing factor.

THE EU BUDGET BREAKTHROUGH: DECEMBER 2005

The European Union held a crucial summit meeting in Brussels in mid-December. This was Merkel's first EU meeting, and it was an important one. The EU budget was a sore issue, and disagreements between France and Britain threatened to get bigger. French president Jacques Chirac had even insulted British cuisine at the June 2005 meeting, calling it the worst in the world other than that of the Finns.

Money was a sore point with all the EU nations. Some countries, such as France and Germany, wanted a budget big enough to have a strong federal union and common policies on trade, agriculture, and technology research and development. Some other countries, most notably Britain, hoped for a smaller budget. Britain had even wanted a substantial rebate on what it had already paid. The French and English had taken to insulting each other.

Merkel stepped into this potential firestorm, and by all accounts was the leader most responsible for putting out the fire. Decision-making within the EU is so complicated that only someone with highly developed analytic skills could create a compromise that would work. Merkel did so. She led the way for a budget that consisted of 1.045 percent of the total European Gross Domestic Product. The deal was good for the next seven years, which meant that the EU would have budgetary stability. She was able to get Britain's Blair and France's Chirac to agree to the compromise, also showing her skills as a deal-maker. When Chirac was served cold cod soup, a British staple, the meeting held its breath to see if he would insult British cuisine again. He simply swallowed and said nothing. All were relieved.

Her achievement at the EU summit so soon after taking office was a wonder of international diplomacy and skill.

Merkel immediately became a world leader in function, not just in form. She was now known to be putting Europe's interests ahead of Germany's. She also showed sympathy for the newest members of the EU, the once-Communist Central and Eastern European countries. She listened to them, and built their concerns into the budget compromise.

FIRST VISIT TO THE UNITED STATES: JANUARY 2006

On January 12, 2006, Merkel arrived in the United States for the first time. The next day, Friday the 13th, she met with U.S. president George W. Bush for 45 minutes without aides, and then both emerged into a joint news conference in the East Room of the White House. They were smiling at each other, and seemed to reporters to be quite relaxed and at ease. President Bush said his first impression of the new German leader was "incredibly positive. . . . She's smart. She's plenty capable. She's got kind of a spirit to her that is appealing." He joked that "we both didn't exactly landslide our way into office," making reference to the 2000 election in which former vice president Al Gore actually received more of the popular vote and Bush more of the electoral vote after a disputed vote count in the state of Florida.

Merkel was, as always, honest and direct. She seemed comfortable on this world stage as she spoke for the first time at the White House.

> This is my first visit as chancellor, heading a new federal government. And I explained that there are two objectives we have set for ourselves. First of all, we would like to strengthen our economic force. . . . Secondly, Germany wants to be a reliable partner to our partners in the world, but also to our partners in Europe.

She would steer a middle course between seeming too much under the influence of the United States and seeming too critical of it, as her predecessor had been. She spoke

Germany's relations with the United States have been shaky since President George W. Bush responded to the terrorist attacks of September 11, 2001 with military action. Merkel has proved herself a skilled diplomat, befriending Bush while at the same time keeping Germany's interests in mind. Here, Merkel and Bush hold a joint press conference in the White House on January 13, 2006, during Merkel's first visit to the United States.

in German, even though she speaks English fluently; some thought this further asserted her independence. She told the news conference the she would make sure President Bush knew where they agreed and where they disagreed. She would not be as confrontational about such issues as the war in Iraq as Chancellor Schröder had been. She had, however, objected to the treatment of prisoners at the U.S. base at Guantanamo Bay, Cuba. She had also called terrorism a most important international threat. She said she knew that European countries also had to devise a clear and fair way of dealing with terrorist detainees.

Political scientists have noted that Merkel and other German officials do not use the term "war on terror." For most Europeans, "war" means armies clashing, not one army trying to fight a much smaller group of criminals and terrorists. German foreign policy did not accept waging war with entire countries because of a few select terrorists as an effective strategy. Merkel, however, was sympathetic to U.S. goals in hunting down Saddam Hussein and toppling his government.

Merkel reminded the group that U.S.-German relations had to rest on much more than fighting terrorism. International trade issues, possible nuclear weapon development in Iran, relationships with China and Russia, troubles in Lebanon, the EU, and much more would be the subject of further discussions. They both agreed that it was very important that they work together.

MEETING IN RUSSIA

Merkel left the United States and soon flew to Moscow to meet with Russian president Vladimir Putin. He met her at the Kremlin and presented her with a gift—a small black and white dog. Merkel had been bitten by a dog when she was a child, and doesn't like dogs. German diplomats were not sure if Putin was aware of this, and so were uncertain how to interpret the gift. Reporters noted that Merkel speaks fluent Russian, unlike Schröder, and so may have been a more able negotiator with Putin on a wider range of issues than her predecessor. Schröder had become known for his sleigh rides with Putin, and his unwillingness to press Putin on difficult issues. Merkel was making a different statement. She would be taking no sleigh rides, at least not now.

One of the most important issues Merkel wanted to address was having reliable energy coming to Europe from Russia's

Merkel's first meeting as chancellor with Russian president Vladimir Putin took place on January 16, 2006. Although the two leaders agree on many issues, and have set up an alliance, Merkel has criticized Putin's energy policies.

natural gas company, Gazprom. Roughly half of Europe's natural gas needs are met by Gazprom, and price increases and scandals had shaken European confidence that it was a reliable source. Putin and Merkel reportedly discussed the issue at length, and Merkel received the assurances she needed.

After her meeting at the Kremlin, Merkel and her aides sped through evening traffic to get to the German ambassador's residence in Moscow. There, she met with leaders from various human rights organizations, whose activities were expected to be restricted under new laws favored by Putin. Merkel wants Germany to support human rights organizations and other nongovernmental organizations (NGOs); growing up in East

SHE SEEMED TO MANY
TO HAVE CHANGED SINCE
BECOMING CHANCELLOR, TO BE
MORE CONFIDENT AND SECURE.

Germany made her realize how important such organizations are. By meeting with the human rights activists, she showed she could be critical of Russia and Putin.

TAKING THE LEAD: SPRING 2006

After her meetings in Moscow, Merkel flew home to Berlin. In just a week she had met with leaders both in Washington and Moscow and raised difficult issues in both places. Her diplomatic skill came as a surprise to many world leaders, who had assumed Merkel's lack of international experience would force her to focus on German domestic issues at first. Instead, she had tackled some the world's most difficult problems head on, and earned the respect of most. Journalist Jim Hoagland of the *Washington Post* wrote "Merkel's clear-eyed realism about both Washington and Moscow makes her an interesting new and potentially stabilizing force of leadership in a world sorely in need of that quality." Gert Weisskirchen, a foreign policy expert in Germany, wrote of the trips that "she represents a new form of body language, of style, and you see that in her Washington trip, and in her trip to Moscow. It's encouraging that she sought dialogue with NGOs in Russia, as well as her willingness to clearly state the European position on Guantanamo Bay." She seemed to many to have changed since becoming chancellor, to be more confident and secure. She had always been cool, analytical, and pragmatic. Now she had more people watching and appreciating her. With British prime minister Tony Blair, Italian prime minister Silvio Berlusconi, and French president Jacques Chirac coming to the end of their long terms in office, Merkel was now Europe's strongest political leader. She had proven she could network in her nation's interest, and also in the world's interest.

A dangerous issue demanded her attention in the spring of 2006. Merkel had been coordinating with the EU and the United States a response to evidence of Iran's enrichment of uranium. Enriched uranium is only used for nuclear bombs or nuclear reactors. Many feared that Iran was developing the bombs and saying instead that it was developing the reactors. Some world leaders were afraid the United States would attack Iran as it had Iraq, and so effective diplomacy, the sort Merkel could carry out, was more important than ever. Germany, France, and Great Britain wanted to establish closer ties to Iran, offering incentives not to develop nuclear weapons. Merkel had suggested that direct talks between President Bush and Iranian president Mahmoud Ahmadinejad might help. But, Washington had cut off diplomatic relations with its capital Tehran in 1979 after U.S. hostages were taken. The United States did not want to re-open talks with Tehran, so Merkel's diplomacy became crucial.

Advances in foreign relations were not the only areas in which Merkel was succeeding. By April 2006, the German economy seemed to have improved slightly, with a national unemployment under 11 percent. There were still more than 4 million people out of work, but the perception within the country was that German companies and consumers were now more optimistic than they had been for years. Some suggested that Germans were simply tired of being pessimistic. Some said the upcoming World Cup soccer tournament was lightening the German mood. Little did anyone know how much Merkel was personally looking forward to hosting the World Cup.

A VISIT TO CHINA: MAY 2006

Merkel knew that close relationships with the United States, Russia, Great Britain, and France were crucial to Germany's foreign policy. There was one more country that she needed to visit in her first few months in office. On May 21, she arrived in Beijing, China, leading a 41-person delegation representing many important German business interests. Leaders from Siemens and Lufthansa and other large German companies were with her to establish closer ties to the world's largest market for their products. News videos show her walking side by side with Chinese premier Wen Jiabao during a welcoming ceremony at the Great Hall of the People in Beijing on May 22.

Business was not the entire agenda. Merkel wanted China to agree that Iran should not be allowed to develop nuclear weapons, and by all accounts China did agree. Merkel's expertise in physics and nuclear reactions gave her a kind of authority to weigh in on issues that other leaders may not have. She was an expert, knew what went into nuclear power plant fueling, and could not be confused by scientists trying to protect Iran.

Merkel also met President Hu Jintao, and then went to Shanghai. When she took the high-speed, magnetically levitated train (maglev) from Shanghai's urban center to Pudong Airport, she must have been reminded of her first trip on a high-speed train to Hamburg in 1986, when she visited for her cousin's wedding. The maglev was made by Siemens, and both Merkel and Siemens leaders wanted to expand maglev train use in China. Maglevs are marvels of modern technology, and Germany leads the way in their production.

THE WORLD CUP, 2006

People walking around Berlin in early June 2006 started to notice something they had not seen for a very long time. Hanging from windows, draped around people's shoulders, and waving from moving cars were banners of black, red, and gold. The German national flag had been seen in postwar Germany, of course, but not in these numbers. *New York Times* reporter Richard Bernstein wandered through Berlin on June 17 and filed a report:

For most of the years since World War II, the Germans have
not really been sure whether it is appropriate to display
emblems showing they loved their country. For decades
patriotism was associated with nationalism, and that most
terrible manifestation of nationalism, blind obedience to
an evil leader. . . . So why, just now, has public sentiment
moved toward flag-waving? Many factors could be involved.
Germany has a new president, Angela Merkel, who has
emerged as possibly the most effective leader among the big
countries of Europe. The economy is on a modest upswing.
. . . Mr. [Gary] Smith, with the American Academy in Berlin,
said the Germans, who are a homogeneous people, are finding it enjoyable suddenly to be host to so many people from
so many countries.

Germany was hosting the World Cup, the most watched
international sporting event in the world, along with the
Olympics. Germans were simply in a good mood. World Cup
fans danced in the streets with red, black, and gold mini-
dresses, jester hats, and wigs. Not since 11/9/89 had Germany
celebrated like this, and many felt this was even more of a
national holiday. Flag sales were setting records.

The connection between soccer and patriotism had a history in Germany. The Germans had unexpectedly won the 1954
World Cup, but when some fans began singing a banned ver-
sion of the national anthem, the world criticized the celebrations as being too close to a Nazi rally. Politicians had to tell the
fans not to cheer too loudly. No one would have to tell the fans
that in 2006 Germany.

Merkel discussed the World Cup before it opened:

There are many dimensions to football's [soccer's] allure and
appeal: top-class moves, thrilling goals, majestic star players,
thunderous encounters and passionate fans. Football stirs
the emotions all over the globe. . . . I'm personally looking
forward to a festival of goals, excitement and fair play. We

Germans will be right behind our national team, but our aim is to act as welcoming hosts and friends to every team and their fans.

She watched several of the matches of the 2006 World Cup intently, and never missed one in which Germany played. She became a highly visible symbol of a nation wanting the best for its team. She loved the sport and the competition. She became a famous fan. Germany came in third in the 2006 World Cup, behind winner Italy and runner-up France. Even though they did not win, the Germans played well and the country loved them. They were skilled, but they were also good sports—no one on the German team head-butted anyone. When Merkel congratulated Italy on its win, she went on to say that the German team "enraptured us with their passion and courage. Germany is the world champion of our hearts." Her nation saw a softer and more playful side to their serious leader during the World Cup. It loved that side to her.

PREPARING FOR THE 2006 G-8 SUMMIT: U.S. VISITORS

After the World Cup, it was back to world business. The major meeting for Merkel in the summer of 2006 was the G-8 summit. The G-8 is a meeting for the leaders of the eight largest industrialized democracies. It started after the 1973 oil crisis as a way of avoiding that kind of critical situation again. The three-day meeting is held in different countries in the middle of the year. To prepare for the meeting, and to keep a promise she made to President Bush when she met him in January, Merkel invited President Bush and first lady Laura Bush to visit her on their way to the G-8. On July 13, the three went with a large group of advisers and security people to a small city called Stralsund, on the Baltic Sea in northeastern Germany. The city is a beautiful and ancient seaport and shipbuilding center—it was designated as a UNESCO World Heritage site in 2002. Handsome gabled houses line the streets. Out of the city, gray concrete housing projects mark the Communist–East German past, but those areas were not on the itinerary.

Merkel addressed a large audience in the Stralsund Market Square, welcoming the Bushes and the American delegation:

> I think I can safely say that ever since we were able to achieve German unity a lot has happened, and, indeed, Stralsund is a case in point. If you look at the fact that when the GDR finally collapsed you had about 600 monuments here of historic importance in the city, itself, that were slowly decaying, that were slowly in ruins, and part of them has been restored over time. But there are still quite a lot of problems that remain to be solved. One of them, obviously, is the fairly high unemployment in this particular part of the country, the need for economic progress and economic upturn. And this is why I am also delighted to have you here, to show you here in my constituency what it means when people try to take their own fate, their own future into their own hands.

Merkel then presented the Bushes with a barrel of herring, making the president and first lady laugh. Then, they all traveled to a small village called Trinwillershagen (it has roughly 1,000 residents) to feast on barbecued wild boar, venison, and duck. Reporters joked that this was the German equivalent of a day at the president's ranch in Crawford, Texas. The village had been a weekend retreat for some Communist leaders, and had remained somewhat popular as a romantic getaway. The local Germans were glad for the business.

The world leaders got time to discuss matters of mutual interest before the G-8. One issue they did not discuss but which made the local papers was the cost of the Bush visit—some $15 million for the 12,500 police officers they used, welded manhole covers in Stralsund needed for tight security, the stands to hold audiences for ceremonies, and more.

Straslund was too poor a city to pay the bill, but the matter would be resolved somehow.

THE 2006 G-8 SUMMIT

From July 15 to July 17, 2006, the world attention's turned to St. Petersburg, Russia. The G-8 summit included leaders from Canada, France, Germany, Italy, Japan, Russia, the United Kingdom, and the United States. The European Union was also represented as a group. The leaders and their aides from the countries gathered in the beautiful and elaborate Konstantinovsky Palace near St. Petersburg. The palace had been built in the eighteenth century for the ruling family, the Romanovs, but had fallen into ruin after World War II. President Putin had ordered it to be completely renovated, and the palace was finished just in time for the meeting. Some now call it the "Palace of Putin."

Since the G-8 countries are both wealthy and influential, they try to address global problems like pollution or terrorism. Critics point out that they are often trying to solve problems they themselves have created, and protesters are common in the cities of the meetings. Putin, the host of the meeting in 2006, had an agenda that included energy security, infectious diseases (AIDS, malaria, and bird flu), and education. The real agenda, however, was determined by world events at the time. Israel and the Lebanon-based organization Hezbollah had renewed a very dangerous conflict, and an open war had broken out between the two. War in the Middle East is one of the most polarizing issues a G-8 meeting can have. Much of the three days was taken up discussing how to help calm the region and restore some kind of peace.

An ongoing issue at any G-8 is world poverty, and what strategies and policies can help reduce it. Each of the G-8 countries pays subsidies to its own farmers and has tariffs on imported food, making it difficult for poorer agrarian nations to trade their way out of poverty. No country wants to change things until all do, so each refuses to budge until all the others do. The 2006 G-8 did not help solve this kind of standoff.

Merkel made G-8 headlines in three stories carried around the world. The first was when she promised that as host of the 2007 G-8 she would make poverty the top priority. Of all the assembled world leaders, she may have grown up the poorest, so poverty was not an abstract concept to her. An editorial in the *Los Angeles Times* said that "Merkel's gesture shows that the campaign to attack the world's most pressing problem remains alive."

The second Merkel G-8 headline was when her friend President Bush came up behind her during a break and began to give her an upper-back massage. Her startled her, and she threw up her arms to get his hands off her. A security camera captured the action, and its images were transmitted around the world on the Internet. Some on the world press were outraged that the U.S. president had acted like "a frat boy" at one of the world's most important political gatherings. Others scolded that workplace etiquette dictated that unwanted touching of any kind was out of place. Some defended Bush, saying this was an accepted practice among good friends and he thought Merkel was his very close friend. In any case, Merkel seemed to make light of the incident later, and seemed not offended after her initial reaction. But, the affair called attention to her position as a woman world leader and how other leaders needed to know that the world had changed from an old boys club.

The third headline was that Merkel had been the only politician either courageous enough or inexperienced enough to criticize the host country, Russia. She took the Russians to task for their electoral system, saying it had several shortcomings. She was vocal about needing energy security for Europe and did not want the natural gas from Russia to get disrupted again. Usual G-8 protocol meant that the host country did not get criticized by the other leaders. Merkel was too honest for that protocol, and thought this world stage was a good place to

At the 2006 G-8 summit, held in Russia, leaders from the world's richest and most influential nations met to address global issues. Photographed on July 16 at Konstantinovsky Palace outside St. Petersburg are *(left to right)* Italian prime minister Romano Prodi; German chancellor Angela Merkel; British prime minister Tony Blair; French president Jacques Chirac; Russian president Vladimir Putin; U.S. president George W. Bush; Japanese prime minister Junichiro Koizumi; Canadian prime minster Stephen Harper; Finnish prime minister Matti Vanhanen; and EU commission chief Jose Manuel Barroso.

call attention to Russian voting systems and also the need for energy security. Some other leaders rushed to defend Russia. She knew she had made her mark at her first G-8.

TERRORISM IN GERMANY

In late August 2006, Germany made world headlines when a plot to blow up two German trains was uncovered. A 21-year-old Lebanese man identified as Youssef Mohamed was arrested for allegedly putting suitcases stuffed with propane gas bombs on several trains. He must have had at least one accomplice, for whom German police were searching. Police found the suitcases with the unexploded bombs on regional trains in the western cities of Dortmund and Koblenz. Using DNA evidence, the police narrowed their search to Kiel, where the young man had been about to begin his university studies.

The bombers may have been motivated by anger at the Israel-Hezbollah war. Germany had agreed to play a peace-keeping role in southern Lebanon as part of an international force. Earlier in August, a plot to blow up passenger planes flying from Great Britain to the United States had also been uncovered, resulting in changes to airline security procedures. No one knew if the two plots were related to each other. Since Germany had not been the subject of any terrorist attacks in the time since the September 11, 2001, attacks on the United States, Germany may have felt immune to the threats. Now, that immunity had worn off, and Germans were shaken.

Merkel did not try to increase fears; instead, she tried to reassure the country that even though constant vigilance was necessary, there was no need to treat this threat as a real war. Germans and other Europeans know all too well what a real war is. She reaffirmed her support for an expanded use of closed-circuit cameras in train stations and other public places. She said, "We must continue to discuss the balance between video surveillance, which I'm totally in favor of, data protection, and the restriction of certain rights." Berlin and other German cities have fewer surveillance cameras than London, and Germany does not do phone-record surveillance as the United States does. The Nazi past makes Germans very reluctant to grant the state that much power over its citizens.

THE END OF THE HONEYMOON: LATE SUMMER, 2006

Merkel's unprecedented high ratings in German polls began to come back down to Earth by September 2006. Many said her honeymoon was now officially over. The unemployment rate was better, but still remained high at 10.6 percent. Volkswagen announced that it was cutting as many as 20,000 employees, and Deutsche Bank said it would be firing people as well. Merkel's plan to raise taxes was unpopular, even though many agreed it was the most responsible thing to do in the face of an enormous deficit.

Health care was also a major and divisive issue. Germans have universal health care, managed under 252 public health funds covering roughly 90 percent of population. The other 10 percent have private insurance because they are either wealthy or are civil servants. The system, however, is under increasing strain because of an aging population, a large bureaucracy, and increased costs. Merkel wanted to reform the system, to introduce more competition into it. She wanted the public and private firms to compete for business. She encountered an enormous amount of resistance, and had to agree to higher contributions from employers and employees rather than streamlining the health care bureaucracy. Again, her efforts were politically unpopular, but many experts agree they were exactly the right economic medicine needed. She did get some of what she wanted—there is now more competition between private and public insurers, and clients can switch companies more freely.

Energy was another issue that demanded Merkel's attention and may have brought her honeymoon to an end. Oil prices rose throughout the summer of 2006, making Germany's energy policy shortcomings even more apparent. Germany relied on natural gas from Russia, and criticizing Russia as Merkel had done made some Germans very nervous. Merkel has been forced to expand Germany's reliance on one of the oldest fuels: coal. Coal is cheap, reliable, and still plentiful in Germany, but it emits twice the carbon dioxide that natural gas does. Germany, unlike the United States, signed the Kyoto

On October 21, 2006, protestors hold banners reflecting their unhappiness with the German government's social reforms. One reads, "Politicians, are you crazy?" Merkel's plans for reform caused a dip in her popularity.

protocols and is obligated to reduce its emissions of carbon dioxide and other greenhouse gases by 20 percent by 2012.

Reliance on coal for generating electricity has had another effect on Germany. Whole villages have had to be moved to continue mining the brown coal (called lignite) in eastern Germany. Forcibly relocating an entire village is disruptive and expensive—and certainly not politically appealing. If a village lies in the path of the needed excavation of the coal, however, there is no other choice if the energy policy remains as is. The Dutch have windmills, the French have their nuclear power plants, but the Germans have their coal-fired hulking boilers spewing tons of carbon dioxide into the air. Even though they have equipped plants with filters and scrubbers that have reduced sulfur dioxide and nitrogen dioxide emissions, the plants seem like a very old technology. Merkel's expertise with nuclear power plants may not help; the mood of the country is to try to get rid of all nuclear power plants by 2020.

New York Times reporter Mark Lander wrote in September 2006 that "Merkel is the victim of eroding public support, infighting in her party, and the need to reconcile the competing interests of a balky 'grand coalition' government, which has hampered her ability to take bold steps." Some in Germany now worry that she is more a moderator than a leader. She has moved quickly to ease those worries. When she returned from a summer vacation hiking trip in the Italian Alps, she criticized her critics. She said the German economy was no longer "the sick man" of Europe.

The avalanche of world events will continue to fall on Germany and Merkel. She is a world leader, however, with intelligence, analytical ability, calmness, and honesty. Events will shape her, but she will shape events as well.

6

A Woman in Power

ON SEPTEMBER 1, 2006, MERKEL WAS VOTED THE "WORLD'S MOST Powerful Woman" by *Forbes* magazine. She was not even featured in the 2005 rankings, a sign of how far she had come in only a year. She beat U.S. secretary of state Condoleezza Rice for the honor. Analysts in the article said her key strength was her "unassuming and tireless networking." She had been impressing world leaders from George Bush and Tony Blair to Jacques Chirac and Vladimir Putin. The *Forbes* article said "Merkel allied Germany with the U.S. to oppose Iran's nuclear activities, and she was vocal on energy security at the G8 meeting this summer." Merkel was the only European leader to make it into the top ten. China's deputy leader Wu Yi was third.

GENDER EQUALITY IN GERMANY
With Merkel's early success as chancellor, many in Germany have been asking why it took so long to have a woman

chancellor. The World Economic Forum surveyed women's presence in the workplace, and placed Germany 28th out of 58 developed and developing countries in job opportunities for women. Germany was 34th in educational achievement by women. Fewer women were elected to the Bundestag in 2005 than were elected in 2002.

Journalist Andrew Purvis wrote an article for *Time* magazine on Merkel and the place of women in Germany in 2006.

> The new Chancellor still appears nonplussed by the male-dominated world she has inhabited since her native East Germany was subsumed into its capitalist alter ego. In the communist world of her youth, women went out to work—and often looked after the house, too. But when the Wall came down in 1989, Merkel found herself in a society that chanted the mantra of the famous "three Ks"—Kinder, Kücher, Kirche (children, kitchen, church)—as a prescription for the priorities its female citizens were expected to observe. Last year's elections [2005] showed how little attitudes have changed since reunification. . . . Some senior figures [in the CDU] withheld their backing simply because they were "unable to accept a woman in this position," a senior CDU official told TIME.

The article points out that career women in Germany not only have to worry about their mostly male bosses, they have to be compared to "earth mothers" in their neighborhoods who nurture their children full time to adulthood. Younger Germans do not seem to be rebelling against negative stereotypes of working women; if anything, many seem to embrace the traditional roles of working-out-of-home fathers and working-at-home mothers. German men have praised parental leave policies for fathers, but few take advantage of them in Germany.

Statistics point out that Germany may be wasting some of its brain power. Only 9 percent of the German university chairs

Angela Merkel has pledged to increase childcare resources in Germany, to free more women to enter the workforce. Here, women work at an employment call center in Duisburg.

in math and science are filled by women. In France, the figure is over 20 percent. Fourteen percent of the researchers in German universities are women, compared to 44 percent in Ireland. Only 6 percent of German university scientists are women, less than half the percentage in Italy and Britain.

Merkel has pledged to do something about all this. She has promised to add 230,000 additional places for child day care by 2010. She has worked against legislation that favors stay-at-home parents over working parents. Many think that the more Merkel is in the spotlight, the more people will see that her style of networking and cooperation can work. Her attention to detail and her ability to listen to others, even when they disagree, has now been called the "Merkel Method" by some analysts. If her government can indeed help women, Germany will prosper more than it has.

WOMEN IN POWER

American polls show that more than 90 percent of Americans would vote for a woman candidate for U.S. president if they felt she was the right candidate. Only 55 percent, however, think the country is ready for a female president. That suggests Americans are not as comfortable with women in power as some other countries. From Pakistan to Israel to India to Britain, women have been chief executives. Entire organizations have been formed to figure out why the United States has not yet elected a woman president. The White House Project is such an organization, which holds meetings and has invited figures such as Hillary Rodham Clinton and Geena Davis to its parties. Davis played an American president on the television show *Commander in Chief,* which was canceled in 2006. The White House Project leaders had urged Hollywood to make a series like *Commander in Chief.*

Some in the White House Project think there has been no woman U.S. president because there are fewer political dynasties in America than in some other countries, like the Bhuttos in Pakistan or the Ghandis in India. Others say a woman is much more easily elected in a parliamentary system than an electoral one. A woman such as Margaret Thatcher in Britain or Golda Meir in Israel only had to be elected by members of her own party, not the whole country. Another theory is that the political pipeline for women in the United States is just too narrow. In 2006, there were only 8 female governors out of 50, and 14 female senators out of 100.

Students of gender and politics say that for a woman to win an election, she has to be seen as tough in military affairs. Thatcher was called the "Iron Lady" partly because of aggressive support of her armed forces; Golda Meir led Israel through the Yom Kippur War of 1973. The lesson is not lost on modern women leaders and potentially future leaders. Certainly Angela Merkel supported the Iraq war, as did Hillary Clinton initially. The president of Chile, Michelle Bachelet, grew up with an air force general father and served as her country's defense minister.

Some say the world is ready for a change of that stereotype, and that a woman in power does not need to be militaristic. She only needs to be authentic and stand for something. In 2006, there were several women leaders who allowed these qualities to shine through. Ellen Johnson Sirleaf of Liberia, Mary McAleese of Ireland, and Tarja Halonen of Finland are examples of a new kind of woman leader: educated, smart, and hardworking, without being militaristic.

THE MERKEL METHOD

Political scientists have tried to define what makes Merkel such a visible and effective leader. Some say she has a method to everything she does. The Merkel method is actually a series of personal habits and instincts that Merkel uses as a leader. The first component of the method is that she studies an issue very carefully. Merkel pays attention to details. She looks at all sides of any political issue, and then tries to understand it logically, like a problem to be solved. She tries not to make a decision without a good deal of thought before. Unlike some world leaders, she does not listen to her "hunches," or first impressions. She finds out what others think, especially experts. She describes her approach very briefly: "I am, I think, courageous at the decisive moment. But I need a good deal of start-up time, and I try to take as much as possible into consideration beforehand." All her thinking does lead to action. Political leaders are judged by their actions, not just their words or thoughts. All of her attention to detail and planning leads to actions that are rarely mistakes. Her actions and her words do not contradict

In becoming chancellor of Germany, Merkel joins an elite group of women leaders around the world. Also in this group is Liberian president Ellen Johnson Sirleaf, shown above speaking to the UN Security Council.

each other. Unlike some modern world leaders, there is very little difference between what she says and what she does.

A second component of the Merkel method is having no grand philosophy, no unified theory of politics. Her biographer Gerd Langguth says she is "independent of ideology." She does not have a definite vision of the future she would like to see. She is not trying to fit the world into a set of values she holds dear. Some of the members of her party do not like this about her. They adhere to values and traditions that have been around for centuries. Instead, she wants to define and solve real problems. She doesn't want to invent problems. She thinks politics should always react to conditions, and change. Sometimes a government needs to lean toward being a welfare state, and sometimes a security state. Grand schemes always fail.

She does not have a grand philosophy of how everything is supposed to work, but she can crystallize ideas into forms others can understand and work with. One of those ideas is risk. "I'm ready to take chances. I see the risks; I don't neglect them, but I don't overemphasize them. I think Germany should be a country that takes its chances." She does not want Germany to ever be ruled by fear of risk.

Even though she has no grand design that she wants the world to follow, she does have a personal history to which she is reacting. She grew up in a planned world in which all were expected to obey. She has reacted to that upbringing by believing in free choice and individual responsibility. She is anticommunist because she saw that the communist world led to fear and scarcity. She looks at America and democracy as a set of better principles, ones that give individuals more say in what they become and what they own. She has said, "I know what it is when you don't have freedom, and so I have a strong feeling for freedom, in comparison to the Western experience where the existence of freedom is normal, and fighting for it is not as necessary as it was for us."

She also may be reacting to growing up with a very strong and controlling father. Professor George Lakoff has theorized in his book *Don't Think of an Elephant* that people's political views are often shaped by metaphors from family upbringing. One view is of a "strict father" government that needs to discipline its children, the citizens. They are not to be coddled. They are responsible for their actions, and the father-government will not do much for them. The opposite view is the "nurturing parent" government, where the government sees its children (citizens) as needing protection from poverty, the dangers of war, pollution, and injustice. Others have taken Lakoff's ideas and expanded them, saying that people with very strict, strong, and even domineering fathers often believe that authority figures are important and that good people are disciplined people. They tend to believe that government should not spoil people with social programs. In the opposite view, people with more nurturing parents (where mother and father more equally shared leadership of the family) tend to be more suspicious of authority. They tend to think that good people are sympathetic people and that governments must provide a safety net for less fortunate citizens. Merkel's political philosophy is not well defined, but her actions show her view of the world is closer to the first model (strict-father government) than the second (nurturing-parent government). In American terms, she is more Republican than Democrat. In European terms, she is more New Europe than Old Europe, having survived communist rule and now wanting less of a role for government and more of a role for private businesses.

Merkel obviously has the will to control events. She likes being in control. She likes having power. She has a positive, almost scientific view of power. In physics, power is the ability to do work in a certain amount of time. In other sciences, it is the force that operates machinery or that drives some system. It is necessary, and part of the natural world. Merkel has said "Before [the wall fell], I also wanted power—power over molecules. For me the point is to shape things. That's what I'm doing now in quite another field."

Merkel can also still enjoy herself. She can sometimes relax and not be in control. In August 2006, she took time to help reopen the famous Admiralspalast Theater in Berlin. Austrian actor Klaus Maria Brandauer (who was in *Out of Africa*) was directing a revival of Bertolt Brecht's *The Threepenny Opera* and showed Merkel the inner workings of the renovated theater. She enjoyed the play as well, saying later that she enjoyed a play about people living on the edge.

Merkel's position has allowed her to travel the globe, and she is working to push Germany into the global economy. Merkel *(above)* meets with Kuwaiti officials on a visit in 2007.

MERKEL POLITICS

The Grand Coalition will limit what Merkel can accomplish politically on domestic affairs for as long as it lasts. There are several issues that Merkel and the coalition will need to resolve. One is employment protection. How much protection will German workers be given? German companies used to be famous for not firing their employees. Now, laws are in the works that will allow companies to fire workers during their first two years with only a notice. Merkel is in favor of having German corporations become more competitive globally, and be able to control their costs of labor more than they have been able to. To a German public used to workplace rules favoring employees, the new rules that Merkel backs are not popular.

How much public spending will Merkel push for? As a natural conservative who believes governments should be smaller, not larger, she is pushing against a very long tradition of German government safety nets. She and the Grand Coalition will fight about how many domestic programs should be funded, and how well they should be funded. If lowering unemployment is a major goal, however, some of the job creation will come from new government jobs, along with new government spending. Merkel knows that.

Merkel's instant success in foreign affairs has raised expectations about what she can and should do. Negotiating a peaceful end to Iran's nuclear arms build-up would be a major coup for her and for the world. She will maintain close ties to the United States, but not be afraid to criticize her ally on human rights and intelligent ways to fight terrorists. She will push for an embargo on arm sales to the People's Republic of China. She will push for a strong and active NATO alliance. She will demand a reliable source of energy from Russia.

A picture of Russian empress Catherine the Great hangs in her office. Merkel says she admires the empress very much because Catherine was "a strong woman." Catherine was a German princess who married into Russian royalty. In the late eighteenth century, she became empress of Russia and ruled for more than 30 years. She is credited with pushing Russia into the modern era with her reforms. She enjoyed a great power,

Angela Merkel has brought great promise and confidence to Germany.

inspiring many women after her. That kind of power is not available to Merkel, but she can admire it from afar.

THE MERKEL FUTURE

Some historians will argue that Merkel has been in control of her career and all has gone according to a plan. Others will argue that events changed her more than she changed events, and she has reacted to history more than she has created it. The truth lies almost certainly in between the two positions.

Merkel will end up leading her country for good ends— increasing freedom, prosperity, peace, and justice—or bad ends in decreasing freedom, prosperity, peace, and justice. If she leaves office using her power to make the rich richer with no consideration of the poor, or to encourage people to become more intolerant of outsiders, she will have failed herself, the country, and the world. Failure is not something she knows much about. If the future builds on the past, and world events allow it, she will empower her people. She will help them to be more confident and less fearful. She will help them to be safe and secure. She knows that the needs for peace, wealth, and freedom actually compete with each other for priority in a government. A leader needs to keep the competition for resources a fair one. She will use world events to crystallize thinking. When Hurricane Katrina devastated the U.S. Gulf Coast and especially the city of New Orleans, the world watched in disbelief as organized governmental action seemed lacking. Merkel needs to reassure Germans that their government protections will not fail. Since she wants a smaller government, and is a close ally of President Bush, she has to be careful not to become too "American" for her voters.

She will continue to be honest and straightforward. She will continue to say what she does and do what she says. She will be self-confident, but she also will be sensitive to the needs of others. There have been times throughout her life when she has been underestimated. Few underestimate her now.

CHRONOLOGY

1954   Angela Dorothea Kasner is born in Hamburg, Germany, on July 17. Her parents are Korst and Herlind Kasner. Family moves to East Germany soon after.

1957   Her brother Marcus is born on July 7.

1964   Her sister Irene is born on August 19.

1973   Angela Kasner receives "arbiter" degree in Templin. She enters the University of Leipzig, also called Karl Marx University, in the fall.

1977   Marries fellow student Ulrich Merkel. They move into an apartment in Berlin.

1978   She graduates from university with a "diplom" and enters the Central Institute for Physical Chemistry of the Academy of Sciences in Berlin in the fall to pursue a Ph.D.

1981   Separates from husband, and moves into apartment in Berlin alone.

1982   Receives divorce from husband, but keeps his last name.

1986   Receives a Ph.D. after writing a dissertation on speed constants in carbohydrate reactions. Attends a cousin's wedding in Hamburg, Germany, and sees West Germany for first time since she was a baby.

1989   November 9, Berlin wall opens. Markel becomes member of Democratic Awakening party.

1990   Joins Christian Democratic Union. Wins seat in Parliament as CDU party member.

1991 Becomes Federal Minister for Women and Youth in Kohl government. Becomes vice-chair of CDU.

1994 Becomes Minister for the Environment and Reactor Safety.

1998 Marries Professor Joachim Sauer, former boss at Central Institute. Becomes secretary-general of the CDU.

2000 In April, she becomes president of the CDU.

2002 Fails in bid to become CDU nominee for chancellor; Edmund Stoiber is named instead. CDU loses in federal elections.

2003 Merkel leads CDU to victory in many regional elections, gaining seats in Bundesrat.

2005 On May 30, becomes candidate for the chancellorship, running against SPD-Green coalition chancellor Gerhard Schröder. On September 18, CDU wins narrowly. Three weeks of coalition negotiations follow. On November 22, Merkel is named chancellor. In December, negotiates EU budget compromise in Brussels.

2006 Arrives in United States on January 12 for talks with President Bush. Later in the week, travels to Moscow for meetings with Russian president Putin. In May, visits China. In July, meets with other G-8 summit leaders. On September 1, voted "World's Most Powerful Woman" by *Forbes* magazine.

2007 Hosts G-8 summit in seaside resort of Heiligendamm from June 6–8.

BIBLIOGRAPHY

Bernstein, Richard. "In World Cup Surprise, Flags Fly With German Pride." *New York Times* (June 18, 2006).

———. "Merkel Takes Office in Germany and Announces Coalition Cabinet." *New York Times* (November 23, 2005).

———. "The Saturday Profile: A Rightest From the East Builds Support in Germany." *New York Times* (August 14, 2004).

Cohen, Roger. "Woman Sets Out to Lead Kohl's Party Out of its Crisis." *New York Times* (April 11, 2000).

Hoagland, Jim. "Merkel's Middle Way; Chancellor Charting New Role for Germany." *Washington Post* (January 19, 2006).

Inskeep, Steve. "Profile: Christian Democratic Union's Angela Merkel." *NPR Morning Edition* (May 31, 2005).

Landler, Mark. "As German Leader's Status Soars Abroad, Her Image Takes a Tumble Back Home." *New York Times* (September 3, 2006).

———. "Germans' Sense of Safety Punctured by Terror Case." *International Herald Tribune* (August 22, 2006).

———. "The Front Runner in Germany Runs Scared." *New York Times* (September 16, 2005).

Langguth, Gerd. Translated by Jonathan Uhlaner. "Angela Merkel and the Two Germanies." Bonn: Goethe Institute, 2005.

Lakoff, George. *Don't Think of an Elephant.* White River Junction, VT: Chelsea Green Press, 2004.

Merkel, Angela. "The Role of Science in Sustainable Development." *Science* (July 17, 1998): 336–337.

Purvis, Andrew. "Why Merkel Is Not Enough." *Time* (January 30, 2006).

Theil, Stefan. "'Das Madchen' In Charge. (Angela Merkel, New Leader of Germany's Christian Democrats)." *Newsweek* (April 24, 2000).

Tzortzis, Andreas. "Merkel Shines on World Stage." *Christian Science Monitor* (February 3, 2005).

FURTHER READING

Bernstein, Richard, and Mark Landler. "A German Contender Is Hard to Read." *New York Times* (May 29, 2005).

Blake, Mariah. "Finally, Germans Can Freely Admit, 'I love my country.' " *Christian Science Monitor* (June 22, 2006).

Dempsey, Judy. "For Merkel, A Chance to Mediate Over Iran." *International Herald Tribune* (May 4, 2006).

———. "Father's Ideals Forged Life In East for German Candidate." *International Herald Tribune* (September 15, 2005).

Hensel, Jana. "Country Girl." *New York Times* (September 22, 2005).

Kornblut, Anne. "The Ascent of a Woman." *New York Times* (June 11, 2006).

Landler, Mark. "Woman in the News: Angela Merkel." *New York Times* (October 11, 2005).

Theil, Stephan. "A Radical Change Agent: Angela Merkel Lived Under the Boot of Communism." *Newsweek* (June 13, 2005).

Tzortzis, Andreas. "Angela Merkel Wins Chancellor Seat: East German Physicist Becomes First Woman to Hold Germany's Top Post." *Christian Science Monitor* (November 11, 2005).

Vinocur, John. "Merkel Bends in Mission as Reform Chancellor." *International Herald Tribune* (April 4, 2006).

WEB SITES

Angela Merkel Homepage
www.angela-merkel.de/

English Version of CDU Web site
www.cdu.de/en/3440.htm

News from Germany, Deutsche Welle Web site
www.dw-world.de/dw

News from Germany, Der Spiegel Web site
www.spiegel.de/international/

Office of the Chancellor
www.bundeskanzlerin.de/Webs/BK/EN/Homepage/home.html

PHOTO CREDITS

page:

INDEX

human nature and, 28–29
  religion and, 22–24
competition, education and,
  26
currencies, 46, 77

Davis, Geena, 98
day care, 97
de Maizière, Lothar, 41, 42–43
de Tocqueville, Alexis, 9, 11
democracy, as leadership
  style, 10
Democratic Awakening (DA),
  41–42
demonstrations, nuclear waste
  and, 50–52
detail, attention to, 99
determinism, defined, 7
divorce, 38
dogs, dislike of, 26, 80

East Berlin, travel to and from,
  12–15
East Germany, move of Kasner
  family to, 22–24
economy, 68–69, 92
education, 26, 33–37
elections, changing time of,
  62–63
emissions, 54, 92–94
energy, 92–94
environmental issues, 54–55,
  92–94
environmental safety, nuclear
  power and, 49–52
European Union
  budget of, 77–78
  environmental issues and,
    54–55
  Germany's role in, 76–77
exercise, interest in, 26–27

fascism, defined, 32–33
Federal Minister for Women and
  Youth, 46–48
Federal Ministry for Health, 48
Federal Republic of Germany, 39
Finland, nuclear power and, 52–53
flat taxes, 71
football, 27, 84–86
fossil fuels, nuclear power and, 53
Free Democratic Party (FDP),
  German politics and, 44
Free German Youth (FDJ),
  overview of, 32–34

G-8 summit, 86–90
gardening, interest in, 66–67
gender equality, 95–98
German Democratic Republic
  (GDR), 22–24
German Social Union, Democratic
  Awakening (DA) and, 42
German Union for Natural
  Preservation, 54
Germany unification treaty, 43, 44
Gorbachev, Mikhail, 15, 40
Gorleben, nuclear waste and,
  50–52
government, role of as campaign
  issue, 71
graffiti, Berlin Wall and, 16
gray mouse, as nickname, 62
Green Party, German politics and,
  44
greenhouse gases, 54, 92–94
Guantanamo Bay, Cuba, 79–80

Halonen, Tarja, 99
Hamilton, Alexander, on
  leadership, 10
Harper, Stephen, 90
health care, 92

115

About the Authors

CLIFFORD W. MILLS is a writer and editor living in Jacksonville, Florida. He has written biographies of Derek Jeter, Bernie Williams, Pope Benedict XVI, and Virginia Woolf. He has also compiled a volume of essays about J.D. Salinger, and has been an editor for John Wiley and Sons and Oxford University Press. He currently teaches at Columbia College.

ARTHUR M. SCHLESINGER, JR. is remembered as the leading American historian of our time. He won the Pulitzer Prize for his books *The Age of Jackson* (1945) and *A Thousand Days* (1965), which also won the National Book Award. Professor Schlesinger was the Albert Schweitzer Professor of the Humanities at the City University of New York and was involved in several other Chelsea House projects, including the series *Revolutionary War Leaders*, *Colonial Leaders*, and *Your Government*.